Ronan O'Carroy

Pelican Books
Psychiatry on Trial

Malcolm Lader, D.Sc., Ph.D., M.D., F.R.C.Psych.,
was born in 1936 and qualified in medicine at
Liverpool University in 1959. He then trained in
pharmacology at University College London, and
later in psychiatry at the Maudsley Hospital.
Since 1966 he has been engaged in full-time
research into the action of drugs used in
psychiatry and the bodily changes found in
psychiatric patients, and he is currently Reader
in Clinical Psychopharmacology at the Institute
of Psychiatry, University of London. His previous
books have consisted of postgraduate texts on
psychopharmacology, psychophysiology and
anxiety.

From 1967 to 1973 he was Symposium Adviser
to the World Psychiatric Association. He has
visited the Soviet Union on three occasions.

Malcolm Lader

Psychiatry on Trial

Penguin Books

Penguin Books Ltd, Harmondsworth,
Middlesex, England
Penguin Books, 625 Madison Avenue,
New York, New York 10022, U.S.A.
Penguin Books Australia Ltd, Ringwood,
Victoria, Australia
Penguin Books Canada Ltd, 2801 John Street,
Markham, Ontario, Canada L3R 1B4
Penguin Books (N.Z.) Ltd, 182–190 Wairau Road,
Auckland 10, New Zealand

First published 1977
Copyright © Malcolm Lader, 1977
All rights reserved

Made and printed in Great Britain by
Richard Clay (The Chaucer Press) Ltd,
Bungay, Suffolk
Set in Intertype Lectura

Contents

Acknowledgements

I am grateful to several friends and colleagues who carefully read sections of this book and gave many invaluable suggestions. However, any errors of fact are my responsibility alone. I am indebted to Miss Christine Durston for her meticulous typing of the text.

The views expressed are my personal ones and must not be taken to represent those of any organization with which I am connected.

I gratefully acknowledge permission to reproduce the following: Baillière Tindall for the quotation from Slater and Roth, *Clinical Psychiatry* (3rd edition), in Chapter 3; Hogarth Press and Mrs Marianne Rodker for the quotation from Sprenger and Kramer, *Malleus Maleficarum*, in Chapter 6; Possev Verlag (Frankfurt) for the extensive quotations from case-histories in Chapter 8; Amnesty International for the quotations from their report *Prisoners of Conscience in the USSR: their Treatment and Conditions*, and from their document on Dr Semyon Gluzman, in Chapters 8 and 9; the *Guardian* for the quotation from the letter from Professors Snezhnevsky and Morozov published on 29 September 1973, in Chapter 9; *Survey* for the quotation from Vol. 21, in Chapter 9; the *British Medical Journal* for the quotation from Professor Morozov's letter published on 6 July 1974, in Chapter 10; Paladin Publishers for the quotation from David Cooper, *Psychiatry and Anti-Psychiatry*, in Chapter 12.

CHAPTER I

Introduction

Psychiatry is the branch of medicine concerned with mental disorders. It has always exuded an aura of magic; but unfortunately magic is not a substitute for firm scientific foundations. A disturbingly high proportion of theory and practice in psychiatry is based on accidental discoveries, or, worse, on unsubstantiated speculation. The classification of psychiatric disorders remains chaotic, and there is contention about diagnosis and even symptoms. Many treatments, especially the older ones, remain unproven by modern scientific criteria, and some, such as electro-convulsive therapy ('shock treatment') and psychosurgery ('leucotomy'), involve major and often irreversible 'assaults' on the brain. The lack of agreement on diagnosis, together with the paucity of convincing proof of the effectiveness of psychiatric treatment, leaves psychiatrists vulnerable to the charge of acting against the best interests of their patients.

A whole area of psychiatry, that practised by specialist psychoanalysts, is equally open to the accusation that its therapeutic utility is unestablished. Does lying on a couch for an hour a day, five days a week, year in, year out, talking about problems, dreams, fantasies and fears to a sympathetic listener who interprets them in terms of childhood hang-ups really help? We do not know.

At the other extreme, psychiatrists have traditionally also had a custodial role. Society has delegated to them the responsibility for ensuring that people who inexplicably do not conform to social norms and cause a disturbance by their lack of conformity are labelled 'mad' and locked up. The massive Victorian asylums on the outskirts of our major cities are built like medieval fortresses, but as in prisons the defences face inwards. Here, locked up with their patients, dedicated nurses and doctors attempt to cope with large numbers of behaviourally disturbed people, and, sadly, they sometimes fail. Abuses occur, as a series of inquiries into various mental hospitals has established, and they cannot be condoned. However, they could largely be avoided if sufficient finance was forthcoming for adequate staffing and facilities.

Nevertheless, the custodial role remains and is most obvious in the special hospitals, such as Broadmoor, where dangerous mentally disordered offenders are kept. The public expect to be protected from these offenders, and the therapeutic role of the psychiatrist must be subordinated to the custodial.

The role of the psychiatrist as society's agent in protecting itself against non-conformity raises the suspicion that abuse of psychiatry could happen only too easily. What is nonconformity? Where does eccentricity end and mental illness begin? What is deviation, sexual, social or personal? Could society, anywhere, encourage its psychiatrists to designate as mentally disordered members of political or religious minorities with which the majority disagreed, and then to segregate such dissidents from society by confining them in mental hospitals? That this does happen is shown by the situation in Soviet Russia.

The Allegations

For several years now it has been alleged that psychiatry is abused in the Soviet Union, and some Russian psychiatrists have been accused of certifying as insane many political and religious prisoners.

In brief, the alleged malpractices are as follows. A dissident is arrested and accused of some political or religious crime. This 'crime' is one not usually regarded as such in Western countries: for example, the prisoner may have circulated typed documents criticizing the regime and suggesting reforms designed to strengthen communism. Nevertheless, such initiative is proscribed by the authorities, so that a crime has indeed been committed in Soviet terms. If the prisoner shows any sign of emotional instability, however slight, or if he has contacted psychiatric services in the past, even in a trivial and brief way, the prosecuting authorities may decide to send him for a psychiatric examination. They hope that he will be regarded as suffering from a mental illness, usually schizophrenia, and be found 'unfit to plead', that is, incapable of defending himself or instructing counsel to do so on his behalf. In that event, he does not appear in court, no defence can be instituted, and no damaging statements are made which filter through to the West and embarrass the Soviet authorities. Furthermore, when doubt has been cast on the prisoner's sanity, his writings, sayings and beliefs can be discredited as the ramblings of a madman.

The charge against the psychiatrists in Russia is that they do not oppose this practice, but appear to acquiesce in it. The good faith of a few Russian psychiatrists, Professors Lunts, G. Morozov and Snezhnevsky in particular, is impugned in that they actively encourage the practice by their readiness to diagnose the mental illness, schizophrenia, and then almost automatically to deem the prisoner incapable of his own defence.

The political dissidents dealt with in this way are committed indefinitely to special prisons or to the special prison sections of mental hospitals, where the conditions are alleged to be even worse than those in penal settlements, graphically described by Solzhenitsyn in *One Day in the Life of Ivan Denisovich*. The political dissidents are treated with sulphazin injections, insulin coma therapy and major tranquillizers such as chlorpromazine (Russian name Aminazin). If the allegations are true, then it is inhumane to treat those deemed mentally ill in such rigorous and punitive surroundings, and it is particularly abhorrent to dose mentally normal people with powerful drugs.

Other countries and their psychiatrists have attracted similar criticisms and allegations, but in each instance involving only a few individuals. Only in the Soviet Union is abuse of psychiatry believed to occur methodically and involving tens, possibly hundreds, of dissidents. Nevertheless, similar abuses could develop at any time in other countries, even those with democratic and open systems of government.

Many accusations against psychiatry concern its economics, both in rich countries like the U.S.A. and in developing countries with limited health resources. Thus, the taunt has been made that the American public receive the psychiatric care they can afford, not what they need. However, this economic indictment can be made of all branches of medicine where demand exceeds supply in a capitalist framework and will not concern us in our examination of political abuses.

This Book's Purpose

I was Symposium Adviser to the World Psychiatric Association from 1967 to 1973 and saw the ethical problems at first hand. Consequently, I have concentrated to some extent on the position in the Soviet Union as the most glaring example of the abuse of psychiatry. Nevertheless, I believe that the situation arose not just because of the Soviet authorities' attitudes but also because of the inherent weaknesses in psychiatry. When a branch of medicine deals with intangibles like delusions, when it cannot agree on diagnosis, when treatments are introduced on insufficient evidence, when its relationships with the law are vague and contentious, it is open to manipulation both from within and from without. Psychiatrists, because of the imprecision of their topic compared with other branches of medicine, do not have the means or sometimes the will to resist that exploitation.

In Chapters 2 to 6, I deal broadly with difficulties in the concepts of psychiatry and problems in diagnosis, treatment and in its relationship with the law; these are the first element in the equation: weakness in the professional topic plus authoritarian society equals abuse. Where possible I give examples of direct relevance to the Russian problem, such as in the diagnosis of schizophrenia. Because the situation in the U.S.S.R. is so well-documented and because I was closely involved in some of the events, I have devoted the second half of the book to that topic, which illustrates how the weaknesses and pretensions of psychiatry can be exploited by an intolerant, totalitarian state. The matters are complex, often technical, and the answers to questions like 'Could it happen here?' are not easy. Nevertheless, I hope the reader will come to appreciate that psychiatry could be abused anywhere and that only by the 'eternal vigilance' of both professionals and lay-people can the freedom of the individual within the legitimate constraints of a societal system be safeguarded. It was because of my conviction that some Soviet psychiatrists are abusing their professional positions and because of my disquiet that psychiatry itself has charges to answer that I was persuaded to write this book, knowing well that others more reluctant were better qualified by expertise and experience to do so.

CHAPTER 2

The Psychiatrists

Lay-people are sometimes perplexed by the differing backgrounds, training and functions of psychiatrists, psychoanalysts and psychologists. Psychiatrists are all medically qualified, having spent five or six years in medical school before starting their specialization, which consists of three to five years diagnosing and treating mental illness. Almost all psychiatrists, in discussing the patient's problems with him, use psychotherapeutic techniques, though not employing full psychoanalytic procedures.

Only some psychoanalysts are medically qualified, but all have undergone a lengthy training analysis and have managed their first patients under close supervision by a senior analyst. The layman's concept of the psychiatrist is really a picture of a psychoanalyst. His patients may lie on a couch and relate their dreams; and a beard and a Middle European accent are not unknown among psychoanalysts.

Psychologists are graduates with a degree in psychology, the science of behaviour. The many subspecialities include industrial psychology, educational psychology and social psychology. Clinical psychologists assess and treat mentally ill people and are often part of a hospital team headed by a psychiatrist.

Psychiatrists in Britain

In 1841 forty-four superintendents of lunatic asylums founded the Association of Medical Officers of Asylums and Hospitals for the Insane, holding their first annual meeting at Nottingham. In 1865 the Association changed its name to the Medico-Psychological Association, and in 1926, by which time it had over 700 members, it received a Royal Charter. For a time the R.M.P.A. was chiefly representative of institutional psychiatry, but with the inception of the National Health Service and the unification of the specialty, a fully representative organization evolved. By Royal Charter the R.M.P.A. was upgraded to a Royal College in 1971. Its present membership is over 5,000.

Almost all British psychiatrists work in the National Health Service. Of about 1,500 consultant psychiatrists, two thirds work full-time in the Health Service; the remainder devote most of their time to the N.H.S., with perhaps a day a week for private practice. The typical consultant conducts out-patient clinics in one or more district general hospitals, but most of his facilities are centred on the area mental hospital, the large Victorian asylum discreetly situated outside the town. Here are found the bulk of the mental patients in Britain, many of whom are long-stay, mainly schizophrenic and the senile.

The typical British psychiatrist is 'eclectic' in outlook, that is, his diagnostic approaches and treatments derive from several sources. Drug therapy is an important aspect, together with other physical treatments such as electro-convulsive therapy for the severely depressed. Social therapy is empha-sized with rehabilitation of the socially and occupationally handicapped. Formal psychoanalysis is uncommon, but general psychotherapy, both individual and group, is utilized widely.

Psychiatry is an unpopular specialty among British medical graduates, and a high proportion of doctors training in psychiatry come from overseas. Of all specialties, psychiatry is the most reliant on communication by words, yet for many of the staff English is not their first language. Without these dedicated people, however, nurses as well as doctors, the psychiatric services in the U.K. would have broken down long ago.

15

Psychiatrists in the U.S.A.

The American Psychiatric Association was originally founded in 1844 as the Association of Medical Superintendents of American Institutions for the Insane. Starting with thirteen physicians, its membership in 1890 was still less than 200. Membership reached 1,000 by 1920, nearly 6,000 by 1950, and is now about 20,000. While the number of physicians in relation to the population has been declining for some years, the proportion of psychiatrists both within the population and within the medical profession steadily mounts.

As with other medical specialties, psychiatrists are distributed unevenly throughout the U.S.A. More than half practise in New York, California, Illinois, Massachusetts and Pennsylvania, although these states contain less than a third of the population. Half the American psychiatrists are primarily in private practice. Almost a half of the remainder are full-time hospital staff, mostly in public mental hospitals.

Most of the 1,500 psychoanalysts in the U.S.A. are concentrated in New York City, Los Angeles (mainly Beverly Hills), Washington, D.C., Chicago, Philadelphia and Boston. Psychoanalysis has influenced psychiatry in America much more than in Britain. Many American psychiatrists, while they are not actually practising analysts, have undergone a personal analysis during their training. Over the past decade, this has become less customary, and the authority of psychoanalysis is waning. One trouble has been the strife between various psychoanalytic factions as to the true repository of orthodoxy. This internecine bickering is reminiscent of religious disputations in the Middle Ages and meetings of communist parties in this century. Another reason for disenchantment with psychoanalysis is its reluctance to relate its methods, observations, and theories to other behavioural and social sciences, such as ethology, so that it has been castigated as irrelevant to modern needs and isolated from the mainstream of human ideas.

Psychiatrists in the U.S.S.R.

The first Russian psychiatric society was organized in St Petersburg in 1862 by Ivan Balinsky, Professor of Psychiatry at the Military Medical Academy. The inaugural Russian medical congress devoted to psychiatry was in 1887 in Moscow; preventive mental hygiene and social medicine were prominent topics. Emphasis was laid on working conditions, especially of women, and this foreshadowed post-revolutionary trends. The Association of Russian Psychiatrists was among the first professional bodies to offer their services to the Bolshevik Soviet government after the Revolution.

The number of psychiatrists in Russia has increased as rapidly as in the West, the present membership of the All-Union Society of Psychiatrists being about 20,000. Russian psychiatry dismisses psychoanalysis as an 'enigmatic, arbitrary and indeterminate method'. Instead it tries to incorporate Pavlov's conditioned reflexology into the evaluation of psychiatric problems and their treatment. Otherwise, Russian psychiatry relies as much on drugs as does Western psychiatry.

One practical difference is the existence of a network of local psychiatric centres in close contact with the populace. These dispensaries provide medical, psychiatric, social and employment help for mentally ill patients remaining in the community. Together with day hospitals, such services are more comprehensive than those in most Western countries. These community mental health services have, however, had one unfortunate consequence. Dealing with mildly ill patients led Soviet psychiatrists to broaden their criteria for illness, often to unacceptable extremes. Some correction is supposed to have followed criticisms at the Second All-Union Congress of Psychiatrists in 1936, but some of the present problems of abuse in Soviet psychiatry stem from these broad criteria.

Psychiatrists Are People

Although this chapter is called 'The Psychiatrists', implying some uniformity, I want to stress that psychiatrists as a profession cover a wide range of backgrounds and interests. Doctors are attracted into psychiatry for differing reasons. Most are genuinely concerned to help ill people and dislike the rather mechanistic approach of other branches of medicine. Psychiatry gives them the opportunity to deal with all their patients' medical and social problems. The lack of standardized diagnostic and therapeutic procedures allows them full scope for any particular intuitive flair they possess. Others – quite few – gravitate to psychiatry primarily because it is a less crowded specialty than general medicine or surgery, with correspondingly greater opportunities for rapid advancement.

Some psychiatrists enter psychiatry vaguely hoping to solve their own personal and emotional problems. They are usually disappointed but find asylum in psychiatry, with their patients, and they often gain great insight into their patients' problems as mirrors of their own. And, like all professions, we have our rogues and our charlatans. More than in most branches of medicine, therapeutic claims can be made which are difficult to substantiate, but they will be clutched at by mentally ill people as the answer to their difficulties.

Because psychiatrists spend much of their time dealing with the outcasts of society – the Skid Row alcoholics, the unemployable inadequates, the severely mentally handicapped – they are acutely aware of society's deficiencies. Western psychiatrists tend to be more liberal than society itself, and to urge increased social provisions. They deal with human frailty and day-to-day problems and seek to help without moral censure.

Outside their consulting rooms, however, psychiatrists have sometimes been insufficiently circumspect in distinguishing between their roles as medical specialists and as citizens with specialist training. The most horrendous example occurred in the United States in the summer of 1964. The editors of *Fact* magazine circularized more than 12,000 American psychiatrists asking: 'Do you think that Barry Goldwater is psychologically fit to serve as President of the United States?' This poll was strongly opposed by all psychiatric organizations, including the American Association, but despite this (or perhaps because of it), almost 2,500 psychiatrists responded. Only 571 declared that they did not know enough about the Republican candidate to pronounce judgement; 1,189 were reported as having doubts about his fitness, with 657 opining that he was fit for highest office.

Presumably most psychiatrists and many other people were astounded to find that about 2,000 supposedly responsible professional medical men were prepared to make a clinical judgement based on second-hand sources such as newspapers and newsreels. Furthermore, the ethical impropriety of allowing that view to be made public hardly needs underlining. The poll was part of a campaign to discredit Senator Goldwater, and it succeeded in disgracing some of the American psychiatric profession as well.

Just to disprove the old adage 'Once bitten, twice shy', the exercise was repeated in 1968 with President Lyndon B. Johnson as the 'patient'. Apparently over 2,000 psychiatrists again responded, but the results were not disclosed, as President Johnson did not seek re-election.

Psychiatrists throughout the world seem eager to assume the mantle of the instant pundit. Wherever a current issue has any connection with abnormal human behaviour, a psychiatrist can be found to comment in newspapers or on the television. Where mental illness is involved it is appropriate to ask a responsible psychiatrist to explain the issue involved. But too often the topic discussed lies outside psychiatry and is more clearly the province of a social psychologist or an anthropologist. Psychiatrists willing to comment pretentiously on these peripheral topics, outside their routine competence, are too often extreme in their views, regarding the brain either as a sort of complex mechanical toy or as a mysterious deadlock of life-forces opposed since childhood.

Yet the real problem arises from the unfortunate and to some unpalatable fact that psychiatry lacks scientific rigour and that its practitioners, by and large, lack scientific training or may even be antipathetic to the scientific approach, preferring to rely on their own clinical judgement. Such observations at the bed-side can lead to scientific advances but can never substitute entirely for a rational, considered approach. General medicine learned that lesson a century ago and abandoned remedies such as leeches, purges and vomits originating from well-established clinical 'judgement'. Psychiatry is still hesitantly setting out on the same road to partial scientific salvation. Even scientifically trained psychiatrists, like myself, attempt to hasten too rapidly along that road by formulating elaborate theories on the basis of insufficient evidence.

Psychiatrists deal with disorders of the mind and hence of the human brain, the most complex of all organs. It is hardly surprising that so little is known of the causation of mental illnesses or of the mechanisms that underlie emotional symptoms or disturbed behaviour. Nevertheless, areas of psychiatry which could be developed on an empirical, ad hoc, step-by-step practical basis are still rudimentary and controversial. In the next chapter some of the difficulties in basic definitions will be outlined.

CHAPTER 3

Psychiatric Disorders

In this chapter I attempt to show the unsatisfactory and unclear nature of such general terms as 'mental abnormality', 'psychiatric illness' and 'mental disease'. To illustrate this, the difficulties in the definitions of abnormality and deviation will be discussed with respect to some conditions commonly seen by psychiatrists.

Neurotic Anxiety and Depression

In these conditions, the patient displays exaggerated emotional responses. In an anxiety state, quite minor upsets in life can lead the individual to experience a continuous, severe, total feeling of foreboding, of something ineffably awful impending. As well as these psychological, mental feelings of apprehension, there are physical feelings in the body – palpitations, sweaty hands, butterflies in the stomach, and so on. Thus the individual has symptoms which he can feel, of which he complains, and for which he seeks treatment. We have all experienced such feelings ourselves in frightening situations, before examinations or interviews. Often, in moderation, these feelings have sharpened our wits and helped us give of our best. Occasionally, though, the anxiety became overwhelming and interfered with and disorganized our efforts. But we accepted even the latter as normal for us. Only when anxiety becomes so severe, protracted or all-pervasive that the individual can no longer tolerate it and seeks medical help can he be said to be suffering from a mental disorder, a psychiatric 'dis-ease'. The state of anxiety is abnormal for that individual. He usually feels calm, and the anxiety is a persistent departure from his normal state.

Surveys have shown that for every person who feels anxious and consults his doctor, another two people also feel anxious but, for a variety of reasons, have not sought medical advice. These individuals are 'dis-eased' but not to the extent of labelling themselves as patients by seeing their doctors. This is a practical, operational distinction, not a medical one. Often these people eventually seek medical advice, not because their symptoms worsen but because they become aware of the existence of effective treatments.

Other surveys, mainly in the United States, have purported to show that the majority of the population are mentally abnormal in some way. The concept of abnormality becomes so broad that anyone feeling a bit miserable or tense, not sleeping a full satisfying eight hours or overeating is designated abnormal. Part of the problem reflects confusion over the term 'normal', which can be used in a statistical sense or an idealistic sense, but not both simultaneously. Take dental caries as an example. It is so rife in Western societies that the statistical norm is for a person to have affected teeth. Very few people have perfect teeth, and they are the statistically abnormal. However, from the ideal viewpoint, or from that of the dental pathologist, carious teeth are abnormal because they are imperfect. Similarly with mental health: it is uncommon to have no trivial symptoms or niggling problems. Consequently the statistical norm is for an individual to have some difficulties. But it is unjustified to label such people mentally ill unless their symptoms occasion them so much distress that they seek advice from their doctors.

Furthermore, a mental abnormality may even be beneficial to the individual. A 'photographic memory' is very uncommon and as such statistically abnormal; it is also very useful, and the fortunate possessor will make no complaints.

The ethical problems with neuroses are fairly minor. The patient has *symptoms* which lead him to *seek* help. No one tries to force him to accept treatment. Nevertheless, an abuse can occur when the abnormality is equated with illness or disorder, especially when artificial norms are suggested. Some advertisements for patent medicines, vitamin preparations, health foods and so on imply that perfect mental and physical health can be attained with the aid of these products; the normality of mild emotional and bodily disturbances is ignored. The general public arrive at unreal self-expectations and then entreat their doctors to rectify an imaginary abnormality. For example, people need less sleep as they get older; but general practitioners are importuned to prescribe sleeping pills, with the result that more than one in ten of the elderly now take them regularly. Then withdrawal symptoms and disturbed sleep supervene if the patient discontinues the sleeping pills, and a vicious circle is established.

To summarize, in neuroses such as anxiety states, the individual has symptoms, seeks treatment and suffers from a mental disorder. It is a personal illness; society is not disturbed by it other than to provide facilities for treatment. Other individuals have symptoms and suffer from a mental disorder but do not solicit treatment. Society does not force them to seek help; indeed, medical and psychiatric services would be swamped if all these covert neurotics did reveal themselves.

Psychoses

These are the major psychiatric illnesses that 'mad' people have. I shall discuss some aspects of schizophrenia in detail because of its complexity and interest and also because it is the diagnosis generally applied to the Russian dissidents. In particular, the problems of defining a delusion will be stressed.

Schizophrenia is often misunderstood by lay-people, whose typical concepts are of a Jekyll and Hyde personality or a raving lunatic. Neither stereotype is representative. The term means splitting of the mind: the various functions of the mind fragment and become disconnected. Related ideas become

23

dissociated, emotional expression becomes inappropriate and there is detachment from reality. Intelligence is intact but cannot be used in a realistic, purposive and productive manner.

Schizophrenia is characterized by a wide range of symptoms, which can be summarized under four main headings:

1. Disorders of thinking.
2. Disorders of perceiving and contact with reality.
3. Disorders of feeling and mood.
4. Disorders of conduct.

There is a crucial distinction between the form of a symptom and its content. For instance, a patient may mention hearing voices. It is important to establish whether the voices are clearly heard or indistinct noises; whether they are 'heard' inside the head, or emanate from outside the patient; and so on. These aspects concern the form of the hallucination. The content of the hallucination touches on such issues as whether the voices are accusatory or congratulatory; whether the voice talks about the patient and if it addresses him as 'you' or refers to him as 'he'.

An *hallucination* is an apparently real perception occurring in the absence of an external stimulus, and can involve any sense – hearing, vision, smell and bodily feelings. The schizophrenic patient may be very preoccupied with his voices. We have all encountered pitifully scruffy individuals muttering to themselves on the train or bus. They are usually schizophrenic patients just well enough to survive outside a mental asylum but still hallucinating and self-neglectful.

Feelings of influence are part of the loss of personal identity, the 'dissolution of ego-boundaries'. The normal person is in no doubt of his unique, separate individuality. His actions, thoughts, feelings and will are entirely personal. The schizophrenic patient loses this sense of unity; all aspects of thinking and emotion seem outside his control. Malignant agencies may seem to commandeer his body, forcing him to carry out their intentions.

Disturbances of *thinking* are very significant symptoms of schizophrenia but are only deducible from speech abnormalities. The patient cannot focus on the gist of an argument or train of thought, and irrelevant side-issues become unduly intrusive. The patient loses the continuity of his talk, elaborates on trivia and becomes engrossed in the sound instead of the meaning of words. He has difficulty in using words and phrases symbolically and interprets commands in a concrete way. Warned to 'look out', a schizophrenic may do so literally.

Emotional changes in schizophrenia include blunting of feeling; the patient is unable to respond with the appropriate emotion. Finer feelings are lost, and mood and thought are out of step. A schizophrenic patient may relate a personal tragedy with a bland smile. He discusses his mental aberrations with a superficial, brittle cheerfulness belying the real psychological torture. Schizophrenic patients may nevertheless be profoundly depressed or anxious, and suicide attempts are common.

Catatonic symptoms comprise various disorders of movement and volition. A statuesque pose may be maintained for hours or alternate with wild and sometimes aggressive outbursts.

Consciousness is almost always clear; the patient knows his whereabouts and the date. His perceptions, memory and intellect remain intact.

Most schizophrenic patients harbour *delusions*, key symptoms of mental derangement which have great theoretical interest. Psychiatrists disagree about the definition, or even the description, of delusions. As the diagnosis of schizophrenia may hinge on the identification of a delusional system in an individual, some clarification is essential. As Soviet psychiatrists often base their diagnosis of schizophrenia in political dissidents on the elicitation of 'reformist delusions', the social context of delusions is of crucial importance here.

The usual definition of a delusion is a false opinion or belief. However, 'delusion', like many other psychiatric terms, has also an everyday usage. Thus, we use the word to indicate grossly mistaken beliefs, meaning really that they clash with ours, but not implying that the holder of the beliefs needs psychiatric treatment. These 'normal delusions' may be held by adherents of esoteric cults, religions or pseudo-sciences, but they are delusions only in the lay sense. In return, the cultists may regard others as deluded for not subscribing to their cherished beliefs.

Psychiatrists term these 'normal delusions' overvalued ideas – convictions arising from a strong emotional involvement in the 'cause' but comprehensible in the light of the personality, upbringing and experience of the individual. Thus, the political revolutionary, convinced that social injustice is intolerable, recruits like-minded people imbued with the overriding aim of throwing off 'the oppressor's yoke'. Fanaticism may characterize social and religious reformers who persistently try to win converts and to crush opposition. Although often a nuisance, such people are not mad. Human types vary widely, and they represent one extreme, the other comprising inert, passive, easily influenced individuals.

Less extreme are single-minded people – the dedicated athletes, ruthless businessmen and other stereotypes of this sort. These individuals do not recruit people determinedly, and may acknowledge that their ideas could be mistaken.

The eccentric deviates in only a few aspects of social and personal behaviour and does not usually attempt to convert others to his ideas. Indeed, often he treasures his own individuality and uniqueness. One hallmark of a civilized country is its tolerance of eccentrics; Britain in fact treats them with almost the same regard as it gives to its animal pets.

Delusions are difficult to define psychiatrically. One definition is 'a reality judgement which cannot be accepted by people of the same class, education, race and period of life as the person who expresses it, and which cannot be changed by logical argument or evidence against it'. This definition begs the problem of defining reality, but it contains some basic descriptive elements. Delusions can be elicited only when the patient makes particular judgements. A psychotic delusion is inspired by an absolute and incontrovertible conviction of the truth of a proposition. Normal people may change lifelong absolute convictions when confronted by overwhelming contradictory evidence. Even the fanatic may convert and become equally bigoted in the opposite direction. Indoctrination, coercion, persuasion – 'brain-washing' – cause normal individuals with sincere deep-held beliefs to recant and accept the ideas of their jailers. Only the most robust of personalities can resist such pressures. But, no power on earth, except modern drug therapies, can dislodge a delusion. The shameful treatment of deluded patients in the past exemplifies this. Delusions were maintained despite the tortures of the Inquisition and the neglect, starvation, torments, shackles, bleeding, purges and ridicule of medical attendants more recently.

Delusions often preoccupy the patient, the degree of involvement reflecting the severity of the illness. In an acute phase, delusions monopolize the mind and are easily elicited. The patient broods and is odd and unpredictable. He introduces the delusional belief very quickly into conversation, especially if the other person has gained his confidence. When less ill, the patient may apply himself to his work and reestablish social contacts, but the delusions, although muted, are still present privately.

Another characteristic of a delusion is its intense meaning and personal importance to the patient. Thus one man believed that all radio broadcasts contained hidden messages which he alone could decipher. He listened intently for hours, making copious but unintelligible notes.

These various features characterize the form of the delusion. What of the content? This varies greatly, but it usually seems absurd and irrational. A psychotically deluded patient may be absolutely convinced that a secret gang is spying on him or that he is bewitched, that he has changed his sex or his body is putrefying, that he can read messages written on the inside of his skull, that he is immortal or can raise the dead, that he is Julius Caesar, Napoleon, Hitler or the man next door. The psychotic delusion is seen as absurd, irrational and untenable by other people. Indeed, patients may ridicule each other's delusional convictions, while fiercely defending their own equally grotesque beliefs as fundamental self-evident truths.

Irrationality is a relative and subjective matter. The falsity of a belief can be evaluated only in relation to the system of values held by people in the social and cultural environment of the individual. This may tax the psychiatrist especially with patients from different cultures. A patient's conviction that he is bewitched is not a delusion if he is from a West Indian rural community where such beliefs are commonplace. One West Indian lady I encountered claimed that God spoke to her through the television set. She belonged to a fundamentalist sect, and the advice of its leader was sought. He replied 'Indeed, the Lord God is pleased to talk to us at times, but He never uses inventions of the Devil like television.' The belief appeared strange and irrational to him. It must be emphasized that the content of the belief was not the only evidence of a delusion in this patient. She sat constantly before the television set, cursing if anyone tried to switch it on, and held the unshakeable belief that she was a special instrument for God's word.

To recapitulate, 'a delusion is an absolute conviction of the truth of a proposition which is idiosyncratic, ego-involved, incorrigible, and often preoccupying.'

Loss of Insight

In ordinary speech the word 'insight' refers to the quality by which we penetrate to the essence of things, happenings or people. In psychiatry it usually means the degree to which the patient realizes he is ill. For a patient to have any attitude to his mental aberrations he must be aware of some change in his mind. In many mental conditions such awareness is acute, the patient complaining of distressful symptoms such as anxiety. But in severely mentally disordered states, awareness may be blunted or absent. The patient evaluates his mental state and symptoms with his disordered mind. Thus the schizophrenic analyses the transformations in himself with a mind which has deranged thinking, perception, will and emotions. The judgements and attitudes of the patient cannot accord with ours because his self-observations are falsified and the interpretations of those observations are also distorted. Occasionally a patient denies all abnormalities in himself despite describing bizarre delusions and insistent hallucinations and showing gross thinking disorders. He is judged to have lost insight completely. Usually there is partial insight, the patient commenting vaguely on his 'upset nerves'. One important task for the psychiatrist is to assess the degree of insight.

After recovering from an episode of illness, the patient may regain total retrospective insight, dismissing all his symptoms, such as delusions, as the waking nightmares of a disordered mind. If the patient harbours a lingering belief in the truth of his delusions or the reality of his hallucinations, remission is incomplete.

Implications

Schizophrenia is a complex condition comprising widespread disorganization of mental functions leading to symptoms and to disturbed behaviour. In some cases the symptoms predominate, and although insight may be partly lost, the patient senses something is wrong and seeks medical help. In other instances, the schizophrenic individual behaves in a socially unacceptable way and this brings him to the notice of the psychiatrist; often the patient's family has become concerned about his conduct. With complete loss of insight, the patient may protest his sanity and deny any illness. If a constellation of features characteristic of schizophrenia is present, the patient is labelled 'schizophrenic' and usually admitted to hospital and treated. However, as will be seen in the next chapter, psychiatrists disagree about what is the 'typical' constellation.

A major problem arises in individuals with muted disturbances, such as single delusions. We have seen that a delusion is not easily defined. There are no tests for it, no thermometers or X-rays. The diagnosis of a delusion, with all the implications that follow, is an opinion given by a psychiatrist. In the light of his training and experience he must judge both the form and the content of the expressed idea against the background of the patient's social norms. No one can prove the psychiatrist wrong, but, conversely, he cannot prove himself right. The lack of exactness and the subjective nature of the definition of a delusion provides a loophole which the unscrupulous psychiatrist, encouraged by an authoritarian regime, can exploit to remove from society those who express minority views.

Personality Disorders

This group of conditions is the most ill-defined of all, the most dependent on personal and social norms. At one extreme are individuals with lifelong symptoms who seek help. Earlier in this chapter I discussed patients with anxiety states who had previously been calm or who had tolerated their symptoms until an increase in their severity led them to seek help. Patients with abnormally anxious personalities, on the other hand, have always been fearful. They were timid children and bashful adolescents, and every new experience in life was a torture of anticipation. They seek help because they come to appreciate that they are abnormal compared with their calmer colleagues. However, it is a matter of opinion where normality ends and abnormality begins; there is no clear boundary.

As the individual comes to the doctor seeking relief from his symptoms, there are few ethical or moral problems. Other personality deviations involve symptoms or distress in the individual and include excessive obsessionality, phobias and depression. Many people with sexual deviations are ashamed and humiliated by their 'abnormal' urges and seek help.

Because the boundary between normality and abnormality is indefinable, unnecessary anguish can be induced. The recent change in our notions of what is statistically normal in sexual behaviour has followed careful investigation by such pioneers as Kinsey and Masters and Johnson. Abnormality is no longer a salient criterion for sexual behaviour. Instead, people are enjoined to follow their sexual predilections providing they do not injure their partners physically or psychologically. Much distress has been alleviated in this way by redefining deviation in behavioural terms and diluting the concept of abnormality.

Nevertheless, if people are hurt by sexual practices of any sort, society insists on treating the deviant as an offender; in particular, it absolutely prohibits children as sexual objects. This is one aspect of the much larger problem of individuals who are deviant by society's standards, not by their own. One such group is the inadequates – passive, harmless people who just cannot cope with life. Another type are those with schizoid personalities. These people are reticent, seclusive, stubborn, often sensitive yet unadaptable. They are heedless of the outside world and shun involvement in the pleasures and worries of those about them. They do not confide in others, are shy and bashful and have few friends. Avoiding contact with others they remain emotionally and socially immature. However, the personality deviation does not usually progress into frank illness, though such people are more prone to react to stress with schizophrenic symptoms.

Yet another type, which is of particular interest here because, with schizophrenia, it is the diagnosis most commonly applied to Russian political dissidents (especially the older ones), is paranoid development of the personality. This personality abnormality is an exaggeration of common traits of suspiciousness, hostility, fanaticism, stubbornness and sensitivity, and, as with other personality abnormalities, it is a matter of opinion where the bounds of normality are set.

Chronic paranoid developments are infrequent and usually arise from the interplay of unfavourable circumstances on a predisposed personality; they are usually slowly progressive.

The paranoid reaction may increase the individual's difficulties because it results in inappropriate or ill-advised behaviour, or, conversely, it may help the person. One standard British text-book of psychiatry states: 'Cranks and eccentrics trying to convert society to their peculiar beliefs may respond to the hostility they often arouse with paranoid ideas; but also serious pioneers and *reformers*, who find great difficulty in convincing others, may develop a paranoid attitude, which can be of service in providing them with the fanaticism and driving power to secure interest for their new ideas and eventual success.'

The most problematical and extreme forms of the person-ality disorders, the so-called 'psychopaths', are discussed in the next chapter.

CHAPTER 4

Psychiatric Diagnosis

The thyroid gland in the root of the neck secretes a chemical called a hormone into the blood-stream, where it reaches the body tissues, maintaining their vitality. If the thyroid gland fails, the patient slows down, his mental functions falter, and physically his hair thins and his skin coarsens. The clinical picture is unmistakable, and the diagnosis can be confirmed by measuring the level of thyroid hormone in the blood. In milder cases with less typical clinical features, the blood tests will confirm or refute the doctor's suspicions. Once thyroid deficiency is diagnosed, the hormone can be replaced by administering thyroid tablets; the patient regains his health and can expect a normal life-span. The reason for the failure of the thyroid gland may remain unclear.

Thus the diagnosis of a physical condition, backed by laboratory science, indicates effective *treatment*, implies the probable outlook for the patient (*prognosis*), and facilitates *research* into the pathology of the illness.

By contrast, the diagnosis of most psychiatric conditions is a judgement made by the psychiatrist. His concept of illness reflects his theoretical background, training and experience. The diagnosis cannot be corroborated by laboratory tests or unmistakable changes in the patient. Consequently the 'diagnosis' is merely an opinion that the patient can be assigned to a particular class of individuals with similar symptoms. He will require a particular treatment believed to be effective for this type of patient, his prognosis will resemble that of such patients, and the brain abnormalities presumed to underlie his symptoms will be universal in this class of patient. In fact, it is a presumption and not a scientific observation that the

33

diseases called anxiety state or schizophrenia actually exist.

The way a patient comes to the notice of the psychiatrist greatly influences the process and the ethics of diagnosis. When a patient responds to his intolerable circumstances with intolerable symptoms of anxiety and comes for medical help, the psychiatrist can usually diagnose an anxiety state with little difficulty. The patient is encouraged to describe his complaints in detail – their type, severity, persistence, relationship to external events, and so on. By attaching the label 'anxiety state' to the patient, the psychiatrist is using a convenient short-hand term which signifies a particular symptom pattern, an appropriate set of treatments and a generally favourable outcome. He has also 'medicalized' the problems of his patient in that he is agreeing with him that an 'illness' is involved. The patient is often relieved to know that his disturbing symptoms are not products of his imagination but constitute a disease recognized by doctors and with chapters devoted to it in medical textbooks. This reassurance is the first step in therapy. As long as the diagnosis is arrived at carefully, and provided that the personal, family and social antecedents of the symptoms are not ignored, there are few ethical implications. The individual and the psychiatrist enter freely into a therapeutic contract, and the labelling of the 'patient' is the necessary precondition.

'Psychopaths'

At the other extreme are individuals whom society forces into contact with the psychiatrist. We have already touched on the difficulty of defining personality disorders, but some groups of persons with behavioural deviation are more easily defined: sexual deviants are an example. However, these definitions are solely in *behavioural* terms and do not constitute *medical diagnoses*. This is seen at its most extreme in the instance of the so-called 'psychopaths'. This term has its antecedents in nineteenth-century views on 'moral insanity'. In 1835 Prichard defined this as 'madness, consisting in a morbid perversion of the natural feelings, affections, inclinations, temper, habits, moral dispositions, and natural impulses, without any remarkable disorder or defect of the intellect in knowing or reasoning faculties, and particularly without any insane illusion or hallucination'. Later the idea of 'moral defect' took root, and legislation was framed to deal with unfortunates so labelled. The diffuse nature of the definition and the dangerously wide implications of terms such as 'morbid perversion' are apparent.

In this century the term 'psychopath' was introduced, and, although it is often meant in a narrower sense, the problems of definition remain. Indeed the implications are major, because the concept has remained enshrined in legislation. Thus the Mental Health Act, 1959, states: 'In this Act, "psychopathic disorder" means a persistent disorder or disability of mind (whether or not including subnormality of intelligence) which results in abnormally aggressive or seriously irresponsible conduct on the part of the patient, and requires or is susceptible to medical treatment'. American practice favours the term 'sociopath', emphasizing the social deviation.

Attaching the label 'psychopath' to a patient confers wide powers on the psychiatrist. If aged under twenty-one, the patient can be compulsorily admitted to a mental hospital and placed in the guardianship of the local authority, providing 'it is necessary in the interests of the patient or for the protection of other persons'. The 'psychopath' can be kept in hospital indefinitely if the responsible medical officer deems him 'likely to act in a manner dangerous to other persons or to himself' (Section 44). There is a right of appeal.

The official definition quoted above includes the clause 'requires or is susceptible to medical treatment'. Some experienced forensic psychiatrists have expressed pessimistic views about the treatability of psychopathic conditions, and the British Psychological Society has pointed out that there is 'No solid evidence of the effectiveness of treatment for psychopaths in this country'.

This concept which has bobbed about in the sea of psychiatry for 150 years exemplifies the onus put on the psychiatrist by society to enforce its norms. Although the term has been widened by some to include people with alcoholism, sexual disorders, drug addiction or an inability to keep a job, many psychiatrists, if they use the word at all, limit it to the definition above. Even this is tautologous and illogical. A 'psychopath' is a conscience-less habitual offender who is undeterred by punishment. To *medicalize* this by assigning such people to psychiatric care merely underlines our ignorance of the causes of *social* deviance and the failure of traditional, custodial methods of dealing with it. It is not only illogical but hazardous to infer mental illness solely on the basis of anti-social behaviour. If society cannot understand persistently aggressive or other anti-social behaviour, it should honestly recognize this. If society must resort to incarcerating social deviants in grossly abnormal environments such as prisons, let it do so openly and not delegate the custodial responsibility to a branch of the medical profession endeavouring to maintain some semblance of a primarily therapeutic function. Psychiatry has a useful function in the management of anti-social individuals (as in Grendon Prison) but it must use therapeutic not custodial measures.

In the present context the dangers here are apparent. The Soviet psychiatrists diagnose schizophrenia in their socially deviant dissidents on the basis of 'reformist delusions'. We have legislation which allows our psychiatrists to lock up people as mentally disordered on the basis of anti-social behaviour. But the terms used in both instances are uncomfortably similar.

Socially deviant acts may be more 'objective' than socially deviant ideas, but there is no clear boundary. We could easily stumble or be pushed into abuse of psychiatry with psychopathy rather than schizophrenia as the 'diagnosis'. The Report of the Committee on Mentally Abnormal Offenders (the 'Butler Report') agreed that there was much to be said for urging Parliament formally to disown the term because of the stigma of the label. But it is the powers which the label confers on the labeller which are most disquieting.

To summarize, the concept of psychopathy is really part of the general strivings by an increasingly secular society to replace moral explanations of deviant behaviour by pseudo-scientific terms and to shuffle off on to medical people the responsibility for coping with such behaviour. Not surprisingly, some psychiatrists avoid the term completely, preferring to describe the individual's problems in terms of his symptoms and his socially unacceptable behaviour, and subsuming the entire concept under the rubric of the personality disorders. Many jurists are equally dissatisfied with the concept and point out that in Scotland and Northern Ireland the term 'psychopathy' has not been found necessary in legislation.

Schizophrenia

With schizophrenia, diagnostic problems are more acute, and because of their crucial relevance to the Russian situation they will be detailed here. Although the patient may be capable of describing the peculiar things going on in his mind, he may still have lost insight. He may not seek treatment but be sent by society because of his disturbing behaviour. As most psychiatrists believe in the existence of a medical condition labelled 'schizophrenia', the issue cannot be evaded (as it can with psychopathy) by refusing to apply the label. Of course, the belief may be unfounded; schizophrenia may prove to be an equally dubious concept. In our present state of knowledge there are more advantages than disadvantages in making the diagnosis, rather than merely formulating each patient's predicament in terms of his symptoms, the strengths and weaknesses of his character, the stresses he endures, and so on.

One major purpose of diagnosis is to select the appropriate treatment. Treatments for schizophrenia are only symptomatic and, since many symptoms in schizophrenic patients also occur in other categories of patient, diagnosis cannot be related closely to treatment. Nevertheless, establishing the diagnosis of schizophrenia suggests a course of treatment differing from that used in depression, so that some selection of treatment occurs.

Another purpose of diagnosis is to predict the outcome. The prognosis in schizophrenic patients is uncertain but usually more serious than in depressed patients. Indeed, assessment of outcome is one way of strengthening the validity of the concept of schizophrenia.

A third function of diagnosis is to advance research into the causes of an illness. If mental illnesses are assumed to have many causes, it is unprofitable to search for the same biochemical aberration or abnormal family structure in every patient. Guesses are made about the most fruitful research strategy in each diagnostic category. Usually researchers start with a very narrow concept of an illness, the 'core' cases, and move into less well-defined areas later.

One of the disadvantages in making a diagnosis of schizophrenia is that the labelling has legal implications: for example, some countries will not admit immigrants with this diagnosis. The term can also be used pejoratively and carry a stigma.

Difficulties in diagnosis

As we saw earlier, features of schizophrenia such as delusions are not easy to define and are a source of disagreement among psychiatrists. Furthermore, the features necessary to make the diagnosis are not standardized. If one psychiatrist opines that delusions of thought interference are essential for the diagnosis of schizophrenia, he will exclude many patients included by his colleagues. If another psychiatrist regards any socially deviant individual as suffering from schizophrenia, his concept embraces many people that his colleagues would merely designate odd. No concept of schizophrenia can be claimed as the 'right' one, since there are no independent validation criteria. However, it can be established whether one psychiatrist's concept of schizophrenia is out of step with those of his colleagues, either too inclusive or too exclusive in comparison with theirs. On a larger scale it can be decided whether a school of psychiatry is consonant with other centres in the same country and whether national practice coincides with that in other countries.

The diagnosis of schizophrenia hinges on both cross-sectional observations and biographical data. The former consists of the current symptoms and behaviour of patient. Some symptoms – for example, thought disorder – are afforded much greater weight than others. Longitudinal observations relate to the time-course of the illness, the number of attacks and the social and psychological status between attacks. As both the observations and the interpretation of them are open to bias it is hardly surprising that diagnostic practices differ greatly among countries. Two studies showing these cross-national variations will be outlined.

The U.S./U.K. Diagnostic Project

Diagnostic concepts of schizophrenia in the United Kingdom are closer to those of continental Europe than to those of the United States. European practice employs, by and large, an empirical clinical approach in which symptoms are enumerated, clusters of symptoms distinguished, and the eventual outcome of patients with these symptom-clusters charted. The United States favours the psychosocial approach, which relates the patient to his environment. The psychoanalytic approach, which is still influential in the U.S.A., emphasizes the patient's psychological processes and their antecedents. Rather than distinguishing 'normal psychology' from 'abnormal' symptoms, both psychosocial and psychoanalytic approaches focus on the parallels between normal and schizophrenic thought-processes. American psychiatrists believe

39

that schizophrenic symptoms are potentially intelligible although an extreme form of human behaviour. Once symptoms and behaviour are visualized along a dimension of normality–abnormality, the point at which the label 'schizophrenic' is attached becomes arbitrary. Thus the American psychiatrist may suspect 'schizophrenia' in a patient who is anxious in company, has some odd ideas and keeps others at a distance. It is assumed that processes which occur in the severely psychotic patient are also operating, albeit weakly, in this individual.

Careful epidemiological studies showed schizophrenia to be more frequently diagnosed in American localities than in Britain. To investigate this, the Cross-National Project for the Study of the Diagnosis of Mental Disorders in the United States and the United Kingdom (U.S./U.K. Diagnostic Project) was instituted in 1965. Based in New York and London, this research project developed techniques for standardizing diagnostic interviews, set up working definitions of symptoms and behaviour and utilized sophisticated statistical techniques to classify symptoms and patients.

Hundreds of patients in mental hospitals in New York and London were interviewed in a uniform way by a project psychiatrist to detail their mental state and psychiatric histories. The hospital psychiatrists' diagnoses were unknown to the project psychiatrists, who reached their own standardized diagnoses after reviewing all information gathered by the team.

When the *project* psychiatrists' diagnoses of patients newly admitted to public mental hospitals in London and New York were analysed, the proportions of patients diagnosed schizophrenic were the same. Thus psychiatrists with the same standard concept of schizophrenia diagnose it equally frequently in London and New York. However, when these same patients were compared in terms of the *hospital* psychiatrists' diagnoses, patients had been labelled schizophrenic twice as frequently in New York as in London. In London differences of opinion between project and hospital psychiatrists showed no consistent bias. In New York, when the project psychiatrists diagnosed schizophrenia, the hospital psychiatrists were almost always in agreement; but in addition the latter diagnosed schizophrenia in many patients deemed by the project psychiatrists to display depression, mania or odd personalities.

American psychiatrists have a broader concept of schizophrenia and equate it with severer symptoms. They concentrate on certain symptoms regarded as particularly salient, and they diagnose depression or a personality disorder only when they are satisfied that they have excluded schizophrenia: they use a sequential decision process. The British psychiatrist with his narrower concept is more concerned with the overall clinical picture than the type of symptoms. He uses a parallel decision process, diagnosing schizophrenia as a choice out of several options. For example, to many American psychiatrists, auditory hallucinations in clear consciousness imply a schizophrenic disease process. To most British psychiatrists such a symptom is as likely to signify a severe depressive illness as schizophrenia.

The Russian Concept of Schizophrenia

The concept of schizophrenia varies among psychiatrists in different parts of the Soviet Union. My impression of psychiatrists from Leningrad and Kiev is that their ideas on schizophrenia resemble the restricted concepts of the average British psychiatrist. The 'provincial' psychiatrists claimed that their views were usual except in Moscow and one or two other centres, such as Tbilisi in Soviet Georgia.

The Institute of Psychiatry in Moscow is part of the Academy of Medical Sciences, the most prestigious organization of its kind in the Soviet Union. It is the biggest, the best-funded and the most influential of Soviet psychiatric institutes. Being in Moscow, it is the most ideologically dependable and sets an example to the provincial institutes. Its director, Professor A.

V. Snezhnevsky, announced in the early 1950s a 'Pavlovian theory of schizophrenia' with a very broad concept of schizophrenia.

Professor Snezhnevsky and his school, as Marxists, concentrate on the social antecedents and consequences of mental illness. One beneficial outcome has been the provision of excellent rehabilitation services for the mentally ill. However, this school emphasizes the social adjustment and the course of the illness while underplaying the detailed symptom form and content of the illness. Thus, R. A. Nadzharov of the Moscow school stated explicitly in 1972 that examination of the type and rate of disease process in schizophrenia led to the rejection of the usual concepts of schizophrenia based on symptom assessments.

Whatever the reasons, the prevalence of schizophrenia (that is, the number of individuals with that diagnosis) in Moscow is about twice that found in British studies.

A crucial major difference between the Moscow school and the rest of Europe is the propensity of the Russians to label a patient 'schizophrenic' because of deviant ideas, both for the insistency of his views and for the content of the ideas. Moscow psychiatrists seem to diagnose schizophrenia even if symptoms are minimal. Thus Snezhnevsky and Vartanian write: 'Among the cases of continuous schizophrenia there are patients who have quite rudimentary phenomena with a very slow development of the process, a non-progressive course, an incompletely developed variety of the disease'. Also, they aver, 'The varieties of diseases are practically inexhaustible'. With such wide concepts of schizophrenia, almost anyone showing deviation of any sort is in danger of being diagnosed as schizophrenic. We shall see how social deviance in the U.S.S.R. comes to be regarded as an illness when we consider the case-histories of some of the dissidents.

The International Pilot Study of Schizophrenia

Evidence that the Moscow view of schizophrenia is itself deviant comes from a study in nine countries under the auspices and coordination of the Office of Mental Health of the World Health Organization (W.H.O.), an agency of the United Nations situated in Geneva. The nine centres are Aarhus, Denmark; Agra, India; Cali, Columbia; Ibadan, Nigeria; London, England; Moscow, U.S.S.R.; Prague, Czechoslovakia; Taipei, Taiwan; and Washington, D.C., U.S.A. These centres were chosen to represent contrasting major cultures of the world covering a range of social and industrial development. At the beginning of the study the psychiatrists from each centre met for joint training in the use of standardized assessment procedures.

Each centre identified about 125 patients aged between fifteen and forty-four presenting with major psychiatric symptoms including delusions, hallucinations, unusual behaviour, disorders of thinking, and self-neglect. The diagnosis of the psychiatrist interviewing the patient was recorded, together with the reasons for his judgement. The data from the assessments were used to classify the patients in two ways. First, a computer program was developed which followed the diagnostic decisions generally taken in Western Europe. Secondly, complex statistical manipulations grouped patients in the study into clusters according to their symptom patterns. This approach presupposes no diagnostic groups but analyses the data by strict mathematical rules.

Of a total of 1,202 patients examined, 811 were diagnosed schizophrenic by the local psychiatrist. The most characteristic symptoms, common to all nine centres, were loss of insight, feeling of being controlled by outside forces, and flatness of emotional response.

Psychiatrists in all centres, but particularly Moscow and Washington, diagnosed schizophrenia more often than did the computer. Indeed, twenty-nine of the seventy-seven patients diagnosed schizophrenic in Moscow and seventeen out of seventy-nine in Washington were diagnosed otherwise by the computer following Western European criteria. The corresponding figures for London and Aarhus were one out of ninety-five and four out of seventy-one respectively.

The empirical statistical clustering technique yielded complex results, one drawback being that it weighted all symptoms equally, unlike clinical practice. This method picked out clusters corresponding roughly to the major clinical categories, thus identifying in another way patients with symptoms appropriately labelled 'schizophrenic'.

A group of 306 patients was deemed schizophrenic by all three separate methods of classification – original clinical diagnosis, computer diagnosis and cluster analysis. By exclusion 505 patients had been diagnosed schizophrenic by the local psychiatrists but not by the computer program or the cluster analysis. In both Moscow and Washington more than four out of five patients diagnosed schizophrenic were the subject of disagreement; in London and Cali less than half were discrepant.

Thus most areas of the United States and the Moscow region of the U.S.S.R. are served by psychiatrists with much wider concepts of schizophrenia than those of their colleagues in Western Europe, and, indeed, elsewhere. American psychiatrists include under the label of schizophrenia patients who elsewhere would be categorized as suffering from depression, mania, neuroses or personality disorders. Similar labels might be applied to many of the patients diagnosed as schizophrenics by Moscow psychiatrists. However, if the assertions of Snezhnevsky and Vartanian mentioned earlier truly reflect Soviet clinical practice, some patients with this diagnosis would be pronounced mentally healthy by British psychiatrists.

Illustrative Cases

At this juncture the reader may find it helpful to read about two patients I treated in the past. The complexity and variety of symptoms will be evident and may help to convey the essence of diagnostic problems confronting the psychiatrist. Naturally, I have altered the biographical details, but the clinical features themselves are unchanged.

Mr H.P., aged twenty-two, was illegitimate and until the age of eleven he was lodged in orphanages. He was then fostered out to Mr and Mrs K. who provided him with a good home. He kept in touch with his foster parents and spoke of them affectionately. However, he rowed with his foster brothers and sisters, especially with the youngest brother, who was about his own age.

The only subjects in which he excelled at his secondary school were physical training and carpentry. He left school at fifteen and was apprenticed as a carpenter for two years. He enlisted for ten years in the army, where he became a physical training instructor and later an expert in unarmed combat. He enjoyed the army, 'especially the brutality and giving orders'. After four years he was discharged with ignominy for persistent insubordination to officers, although for the first three years his conduct had been exemplary. For a year he worked as a labourer in a series of jobs, staying successively shorter periods in each one.

He had many homosexual experiences from the age of nine, but insisted that he had been totally heterosexual for two years before admission to hospital. He claimed many close friends, both male and female, but his landlady maintained that he rarely went out or received visitors. His foster parents stated that he had been popular at school and immediately after, but had been friendless since leaving the army.

He first came to the out-patients department of a mental hospital to seek reassurance about his change in sexual orientation. He was reticent and somewhat odd but without definite signs of any mental illness, and was easily reassured.

A year later he became increasingly withdrawn and resentful. At work he muttered to his mates that their jealousy barred him from the best jobs, and he accused his landlady of searching his room.

After an outburst at work in which he threatened his overseer, he disappeared for two days until found by the police in a dishevelled state in front of Buckingham Palace. He was marching in step with the foot-guards demanding to be taken to the Queen. Instead he was hauled off to a psychiatric observation ward.

For the first two days he was quiet, polite and cooperative. Apart from a peculiar, stereotyped rolling movement of the head accompanied by a grimace, he behaved normally, but was very reticent and uncommunicative in speech.

By the fourth day, Mr P. was restless, pacing up and down, and rude to other patients who tried to interrupt him. Once he tossed another patient over his shoulder with a judo throw, luckily without hurt. He accused all the male staff of being homosexual and of soliciting him and asked repeatedly to phone the Queen.

Noisy maintenance work was going on in the hospital, to which he listened intently. He said that the hammer-blows meant 'You're getting better, Harry', the sawing said 'Keep at it, Harry, you're doing fine', and so on. He was irritable, moody and depressed at times, at other times quite cheerful or even banally giggly.

The patient claimed that it was suddenly obvious to him that he was a V.I.P., that he was 'meant for a place in Society'. 'I am a star. I possess a star. I can stare into the sun without being blinded; I've got very special eyes – V.I.P. eyes, in fact.'

The patient accused me of influencing him by recording his pulse during the physical examination. 'Because the pulse is transmitted to the mind, you can tell my thoughts.' Asked why he rolled his head repeatedly, he explained 'I'm bunged up with other people's life. They're penetrating my body. They have to vomit but they can't, so they make me vomit for them. That's when my neck moves. I don't want to be sick for them, nor spit nor cough. Why can't they do it themselves – leave me alone. Cars and buses say 'Kill yourself, Harry." But I won't. Where do I end and cars start?'

The patient heard many voices and could 'feel' a female patient biting his neck. He knew who and where he was and the date and had some knowledge of recent events.

During his hospital stay, Mr P. had several episodes of aggressive shouting without physical attack. Gradually with treatment with tranquillizers he became quieter but still had truculent phases. He evinced more interest in his carpentry work, which occupied him for several hours a day. He became increasingly withdrawn and unsociable, though, explaining that he had to remain aloof to avoid being dissolved into the other patients when in a group. This sense of loss of personal identity was his most troublesome and persistent symptom. Another symptom was the feeling that thoughts entered his mind 'like a bolt battering on my skull'.

The patient's illness remained unpredictable, with episodes of quiet, cooperative behaviour alternating with truculent outbursts, culminating in the patient bursting into tears and crying in anguish at the unfathomable fragmentation of his thoughts and actions.

Mr P. was transferred to a rehabilitation ward with plans to discharge him to sheltered lodgings or a hostel, with a job as a carpenter. Each time, the strains of outside life overwhelmed him and he relapsed, fortunately without actually harming anyone. For the past ten years Mr P. has been in a long-stay ward in the hospital. He still hears voices but they are fairly sympathetic to him; he still has trouble maintaining his own sense of identity when in company: despite different types of medication he is chronically ill.

Comment

This severely ill schizophrenic patient shows many of the typical symptoms of schizophrenia. Of the 'first-rank' symptoms, bodily feelings of influence, thought interference and bizarre delusions were most prominent. The loss of ego-boundaries was particularly pronounced and tormented the patient. Catatonic features (the head movements), hebephrenic components (the inappropriate moods) and paranoid elements were present simultaneously.

The onset of the attack was abrupt but had been presaged for two years, as his insubordination in the army and fecklessness since discharge were out of character. The progress of the illness was remorseless and the outcome tragic.

There can be very few psychiatrists in the world who would not diagnose Mr H.P. as suffering from severe chronic schizophrenia of undifferentiated type.

Miss W.F.J.'s parents lived in the North of England; her father was a master builder. Both parents were pleasant and sociable. No members of the family had suffered from mental illnesses.

The patient had an uneventful early life but was not robust. Academically, she did not fulfil her early promise, obtaining only two A-levels. She was musical, playing the violin in the school orchestra, but had few close friends.

After leaving school she trained briefly to be a shorthand typist but soon lost interest. She re-sat her A-levels successfully and enrolled as a language student at her local university. She was lonely at university, and so engrossed in her work that she found no time for leisure interests. She became increasingly unsettled during her three-year course, failed her final examinations and left university without a degree. She drifted down to London and worked as a clerical officer in the Civil Service, where her knowledge of languages was useful. Her work was exemplary and she was commended by her superiors.

Her main interest being German literature, she regularly attended a club in London devoted to this topic. She had several acquaintances but no friends and had never been asked out on a date. She had no homosexual tendencies and wished she was less shy and awkward in male company. Her acquaintances regarded her as lugubrious, sardonic and shy, but not quarrelsome or irritable.

The patient studied Zen Buddhism for about a year, regarding it as a holistic philosophical concept with which to gain self-insight. Two weeks before admission to hospital, she 'achieved complete unity – no awareness of outside things'. However, she became increasingly depressed and anxious. Feeling that her mind was sick, she sought medical help.

She spent the first two days after admission in bed, crying most of the time, but then became more composed and discussed her difficulties. Physically Miss J. was almost gaunt, and schoolgirlish and immature in manner. She became relaxed and friendly and quickly established an easy, informal relationship with the medical and nursing staff. She helped on the ward and was kind and considerate to the other patients, being interested in their problems but not intrusive. Some members of the nursing staff and her occupational therapist could not detect any psychiatric abnormality.

During interviews she was cooperative and answered all questions promptly but somewhat discursively and pedantically. Occasionally, she chuckled before replying but always explained the private joke in a reasonable way. Her interest in Zen was dismissed as an escape mechanism to avoid confronting her real problems like shyness. Zen had led her 'into strange regions of philosophical thought', putting her 'under tremendous strain'. She cried with the relief of being in hospital and engaged with more mundane matters than Zen. Neither depressed nor anxious at this juncture, she had no definite delusions nor strange ideas; her philosophical thoughts were expressed vaguely but were neither singular nor bizarre. She denied hallucinatory experiences and any feeling that her thoughts were altered or influenced. On formal testing her intelligence was high and her intellectual capacities intact. Asked how she viewed her illness, she replied 'I've been neurotic all my life and then I may have got into a psychotic state. I was living in a world of my own.'

After a few weeks' asylum in hospital, Miss J. felt sufficiently recovered to return North. She was referred to a local psychiatrist, who arranged group psychotherapy for her. She attended regularly, becoming an active member, sensitive to the others' moods. After eighteen months' treatment she was more assertive in company and tackled her personality problems realistically.

When last contacted, ten years after her illness, Miss J. was still quiet and reserved but was now happily married with two sons. She worked part-time for a large German company as their commercial representative in the North of England. Although occasionally depressed, she had not resorted to further psychiatric help.

Comment

This type of patient presents diagnostic problems with respect to the type of symptoms during the acute phase, the life-history before the illness, and the course of events subsequently. On admission to hospital, she was depressed and anxious, but quickly became outwardly normal. Her philosophical ideas were vague but not bizarre and she did not propound them with delusional intensity. She maintained excellent insight.

Her earlier life had suggested some slow deterioration, with failure at school, inability to graduate and a job below her intellectual capacities. Socially isolated, she was particularly gauche with men.

On discharge from hospital she was labelled as an acute

emotional reaction in a schizoid personality. There is no doubt that in many psychiatric centres schizophrenia would have been diagnosed unhesitatingly. The social isolation, occupational and geographical drift, sexual tardiness, philosophical preoccupation, and fluctuations of mood would have been adduced in evidence.

The outcome was very different from that of the previous patient, Mr H.P. Even the personality problems had been minimized and she lived quietly and contentedly with her husband and children.

CHAPTER 5

Psychiatric Treatments

The ethical problems of psychiatric treatment can be high-lighted by taking examples, as in previous chapters, across the spectrum of disorders seen in psychiatric practice.

The basic weakness is that almost all physical treatments were discovered by accident. The major tranquillizers and the 'tricyclic' antidepressants were found to have effects on the mind when they were developed in the search for anti-histamines. Another type of antidepressant was originally tested as a cure for tuberculosis and found to cheer patients up. Another tranquillizer was first used to lower blood pressure, and so on. Electroshock therapy was introduced because of the mistaken idea that schizophrenia and epilepsy were mutually exclusive conditions and inducing fits would cure the mental illness. In fact one form of epilepsy may be associated with schizophrenia, rather than the reverse. Eventually the use of electroshock therapy in combating depression became apparent.

Conversely, treatments once believed effective have been shown to be ineffective. For many years schizophrenic patients were treated by controlled injections of insulin, which lowered blood sugar; every mental hospital had its special unit giving hundreds of treatments per year. Eventually it transpired that inducing coma with a barbiturate had equal effects. Probably it was the therapeutic optimism of the medical and nursing team that produced what meagre improvements did occur. With the introduction of the major tranquillizers in the early 1950s, almost all insulin coma units were disbanded, although there are still some psychiatrists who believe in its efficacy. They are allowed to continue to submit their patients to a procedure whose effectiveness has never been established. Thus the weakness of psychiatry in diagnosis and measurement of mental events carries over into treatment.

Anxiety and Depression

The patient is anxious or depressed about his life-circumstances and seeks help of various sorts. At the simplest level he would like alleviation of his symptoms of apprehension, palpitations, trembling, and so on. For such symptomatic relief a wide range of drugs of varying effectiveness is available. Some are older remedies, such as barbiturates, but most medicines used in psychiatry have been developed in the past twenty years by the pharmaceutical industry. Examples include the sedative tranquillizers, such as chlordiazepoxide and diazepam (trade names Librium and Valium), and the antidepressants like imipramine (Tofranil) and amitriptyline (Tryptizol). In most patients these drugs produce a worthwhile improvement in symptoms, but do not necessarily 'cure' them; and some patients respond only partially, if at all. On the debit side are unwanted side-effects such as excessive drowsiness, dry mouth, blurring of vision, and constipation. The benefits outweigh the disadvantages, otherwise, of course, the drugs would not be worth using. The patient should be warned of the possible side-effects: too often uncomfortable and even distressing reactions are experienced by the unprepared patient, who then discontinues his medicines but is too unassertive to tell his doctor, who becomes puzzled by the lack of response.

When a patient has failed to respond to the drugs of first choice, another remedy will be resorted to. Such second-line medicines may be less effective in general, or have more significant side-effects, or both: that is why they are not used routinely. The problems inherent in these drugs should be discussed frankly with the patient and his relatives, and the final decision must be left to him. He may well decide that the remedy is worse than the symptom.

The patient should also appreciate that the treatment is symptomatic and not a cure. Otherwise a person with gratifying relief from his anxiety or depression may stop his medication, only to relapse. Very few drugs in psychiatry actually reverse the condition; most suppress symptoms until a natural cure occurs.

Two therapeutic procedures, electroshock (ECT) and psychosurgery, have generated increasing controversy. In the former, epileptic fits are induced by passing an electric shock across the brain. The patient is anaesthetized and relaxed, so that the fit is attenuated to no more than a few twitches. Most psychiatrists are convinced that a course totalling six to eight treatments given twice weekly can substantially improve many severely depressed individuals. There is usually some transient memory disturbance, but the risk of dying during electroshock treatment is very low, indeed much less than the risk of suicide in the untreated. Because of the benefits in the deeply depressed, psychiatrists strongly persuade their patients to submit to shock therapy and try to convince patients' relatives of its worth. At times psychiatrists have extolled shock therapy too enthusiastically and have overstepped the mark; some have even transgressed the law by administering it without the express, informed consent of the patient or his relatives.

Less severely depressed patients may not respond to shock therapy, and in other conditions, such as mania and some forms of schizophrenia, not all psychiatrists would recommend it. Shock treatment was introduced before scientific and statistical guidelines had been laid down to establish the effectiveness of a new therapy. For this, a 'dummy' treatment must be given to a control group of patients, matched as closely as possible to the group of patients given the 'active' treatment. With electroshock, dummy treatment would comprise everything such as anaesthesia and relaxation and the application of the electrodes to the head, without actually switching on the current. An adequate series of such studies is lacking, so the recommendation of treatment rests with the individual judgement of the psychiatrist. He, in turn, is influenced by certain senior psychiatrists who have described in professional journals their experience with the treatment. Too frequently, those ready to broadcast their views are convinced either that a treatment is an infallible panacea or that it is a dangerous outrage. In this way, without dispassionate and disinterested scientific evaluation, a treatment which may have genuine, albeit limited, application and effectiveness becomes the subject of polarized assertions. Some psychiatrists will advocate its use in a wide variety of patients; others will eschew its use except in desperation for a patient who has failed to respond to more orthodox remedies.

With electroshock therapy as with drug treatments, unpleasant side-effects can occur, but in the majority of cases they subside or disappear when the treatment is withdrawn. Only rarely is the side-effect catastrophic as with the thalidomide disaster. By contrast, psychosurgery is irreversible. A cut is made in the front parts of the brain in order to alleviate anxiety and depression. As the brain, unlike most other organs in the body, does not heal itself, the interruption of brain pathways is permanent. The earlier operations carried out in the 1940s and 1950s were crude slashes in the frontal lobes and sometimes left the patient worse off than before, with some relief of symptoms but with disinhibited and irresponsible behaviour. The results were so poor as to persuade the Soviet authorities to ban the operation. With advances in neurosurgery, modern leucotomies involve very limited severance of fairly well-defined brain tracts. Mortality is almost zero and personality changes uncommon. The advocates of these procedures have documented gratifying improvements in anxious and depressed patients who failed to respond to routine remedies.

Psychosurgery has generated intense opposition for a variety of reasons. One of these is that in popular sentiment the brain has displaced the heart as the sacrosanct organ, the greatest glory in Creation. Those who violate it, except to remove blemishes, do so at their peril! Moreover, psycho-surgery covers two areas: the main one is leucotomy, in which the patient is offered treatment for severe intractable emotional disorders; the other, far more controversial, involves the destruction of regions of the brain believed to be involved in aggressive behaviour. The possibility that habitually aggressive criminals might be tamed in this way has led to proposals that many such problem prisoners be offered or even forced to undergo brain operations. In our present state of ignorance about brain function and aggression, such suggestions are unethical.

A third objection is that the effectiveness of the operation has never been established. This has two aspects. First, does the entire procedure – the detailed assessment, the discussion of symptoms, the review of previous treatments, the operation, the rehabilitation afterwards, the careful follow-up – produce an improvement? Secondly, if it does so, is the actual operation an essential constituent or are equally good results obtained with the other less specific elements detailed above? The major problems in designing controlled trials to answer these questions are not insuperable.

So far we have discussed treatments for symptoms experienced by the patient and taking him to his doctor and thence to a psychiatrist. Often the emotional turmoil seems a re-action to circumstances in the patient's life – a disastrous marriage, an impossible job, financial problems. The cautious psychiatrist refrains from expressing his opinion too unambiguously. Instead he encourages his patient to talk freely about his problems until he reaches a fuller understanding of the sources of his difficulties. Then ways of coping with the problems are discussed and the patient can be left to come to his own decisions.

Anyone having power because of a superior training, specialized knowledge and long experience is tempted to use it in what he honestly believes are the best interests of the person who consults him. With psychiatry, the specialized knowledge is still fragmentary and the training too much an apprentice-ship passing on traditional skills. Long experience is not a sufficient basis on its own for the psychiatrist to claim a pretentious charisma. He should share his ignorance as well as his knowledge with his patients.

Sexual Deviation

In many cases the relationship between society, the psychiatrist and his patient is even more complicated, as exemplified by sexual deviation. Sometimes people with problems such as exhibitionism or powerful impulses to interfere with children voluntarily seek help of the psychiatrist. Or an offender who has been apprehended and convicted may then be referred to the psychiatrist for treatment. He may be in prison, in hospital as an in-patient, or attending an out-patient clinic, depending on circumstances. The treatment recommendations may be broadly similar whether the patient comes of his own volition or is coerced by society to do so; but the pressures to accept that treatment are very different.

Sexual urges are substantially under the control of sex hormones. If androgens (the male sex hormones) are decreased or if oestrogens (the female hormones) are increased, male libido diminishes and the danger of a sexual offence lessens correspondingly. Female sex hormones are available as tablets by mouth, monthly injections, or implants into muscle tissue which slowly release the hormone over six months or so. The first type of administration is suitable only for the highly motivated patient who will reliably take his medication. The other two methods are appropriate for less compliant or more disorganized individuals.

Side-effects of oestrogen therapy include enlargement of the breasts, wasting away of the testicles, and possible thinning of the bones (osteoporosis). This treatment is therefore not something to be instituted in a cavalier manner. But even with these drawbacks, many patients are grateful for the relief of an urge which they cannot otherwise control and which threatens at any time to ruin their lives.

The ethical considerations here are more complex than with anxiety and depression. The patient must be fully conversant with the risks of treatment and be ready to give signed consent, which emphasizes to him the care with which the psychiatrist arrives at the decision to recommend hormone therapy. As the treatment is drastic it should be offered only to patients with serious problems, likely to harm others and indirectly themselves. It should make no difference whether the patient is an offender or not; all are entitled to the same quality of care and considerate management. Psychiatrists are not a state-control agency, and courts should not expect them to insist on more radical and hazardous courses of therapy just because the patient is an offender. Public policy and its implementation must not allow the interpretation that referral to a psychiatrist is intended to force hormone therapy on an offender. Psychiatry will suffer abuses like those alleged in the Soviet Union if it allows itself to become an extension of the penal system.

The Inadequate

Increasingly large numbers of rootless and sometimes homeless people are incapable of living in the community because they find it impossible or uncongenial to cope with its complexities. Some of these individuals are suffering from chronic schizophrenia, or are intellectually subnormal or are alcoholics; but many fall outside formal psychiatric diagnostic categories. Most have experienced institutions, such as prisons, mental hospitals, and hostels; others diligently avoid these places; and some gravitate back to them, perhaps committing petty crimes to secure their return to the familiar routine of prison. Nevertheless, they represent no real threat to society, being asocial rather than anti-social.

Many seem incapable of accepting help even when it is

available. They may prefer to sleep rough or to occupy dere-
lict buildings or open sites, or to stay 'on the road' travelling
from town to town but avoiding human contact. Regular jobs
are the exception, but casual seasonal work is sometimes
accepted. Most distrust the officialdom of statutory national
and local authority agencies and are happier accepting charity
and help from voluntary organizations.

Although society and its legislators find such people in-
convenient and embarrassing, provision for them has in fact
been decreasing over the past decade. Many of the reception
centres which had replaced the old casual wards were closed
down, and the passing of the Mental Health Act, 1959, meant
that mental hospitals could not compulsorily detain them.
And as the mental hospitals attempted a therapeutic role
instead of their traditional asylum function, large numbers of
'inadequates' were extruded into an uncaring community.
Adequate facilities are still lacking, yet the need is more
acute.

Public attitudes to the mentally ill became more enlight-
ened after the Second World War, a change encouraged by the
undoubted, if partial, effectiveness of the modern generation
of psychotropic drugs, and enshrined in official policies. In
England and Wales the number of hospital beds for mentally
ill and mentally handicapped patients dropped from 212,700
in 1960 to 174,800 in 1973. Similar decreases have been
recorded in many American states. It is commendable that
the community should appear willing to accept mentally ill
patients in its midst, but such people need special facilities
such as supervised hostels and sheltered workshops. Putting
the onus on local authorities to care for the mentally ill in
the community has led to great variations in provision, from
the half-adequate to the non-existent. We are in danger of
returning to the situation in the Middle Ages, when harmless
lunatics roamed the streets at large.

However, many inadequates do not suffer from a formal
mental disorder and so do not 'qualify' for even the limited
services available. There is nothing to 'treat' in the medical

sense. Yet psychiatrists have long undertaken the care of people who present social rather than medical problems. The management of the mentally handicapped is primarily educational, that of chronic schizophrenic patients social and vocational rehabilitation. The management of the more intractable inadequates is also non-medical, but more clearly custodial, as 'habilitation' is much more difficult than rehabilitation. Furthermore, trying to persuade inadequates to conform and to discharge a 'useful' function in the community has moral overtones of the psychiatrist acting as an agent of society and against the rights of the individual.

Unfortunately, psychiatrists are now reluctant to admit inadequates to their hospital beds. Such people are often dirty and dilapidated, disruptive, complaining and ungrateful. But, most unforgivably, they are likely to need long-term care. The official policy is to contract the mental asylums, and some hospital psychiatrists proudly point to the drop in the number of beds (they seem not to refer to patients) in their wards. Nurses are more ambivalent about the decrease in beds: up to a point their heavy work-load eases; beyond that, redundancy threatens.

Many psychiatrists are deeply disquieted by these trends. Although the number of beds has decreased, the number of admissions has risen greatly, each patient staying for a short time, being discharged back to the community, only to relapse and be re-admitted. The pressures to discontinue the asylum function of the traditional mental hospital stem from a premature and over-optimistic view of psychiatry as a curing profession. The rapid advances in medicine based on scientific investigations of both basic biological and applied clinical topics have led to an over-emphasis in our teaching hospitals on exact diagnosis and precise chemical remedy. But psychiatry is not at that stage, and while it has no new curative clothes to put on it should not discard its traditional mantle of care for the chronically ill and handicapped. Hospital-based medicine is notoriously ineffective in dealing with chronic illness, and general practitioners in the community have to acquire these skills after, not during, their medical training. Psychiatrists have much to teach their confrères in the more 'developed' medical specialties such as cardiology and neurology about the care of the chronically ill.

The tide may be turning. The Report of the Committee on Mentally Abnormal Offenders (the 'Butler Report') drew attention to the lack of provision for inadequates and advocated a 'modest protected environment in local psychiatric hospitals', pointing out that the Mental Health Act does include care and training under medical supervision as part of medical treatment. The type of care does not depend on whether the inadequate has a recognizable mental illness or not, or whether an offence has been committed. This only determines how the patient comes to the notice of the psychiatrist.

However, we must not go too far. Society might want to tidy up its cities, prevent people from sleeping rough, living indefinitely on Social Security and avoiding bureaucracy, but it should not do so by labelling these inadequates mentally ill and deputing psychiatrists to care for them in refurbished Victorian asylums. Only a minority are formally mentally ill, and many can live in the community with sympathetic help. A variety of facilities is needed, ranging from asylums to sheltered hostels, from supervised lodgings and probation homes to long-term social support. Only when a person commits repeated offences and rejects all attempts to help him should prison be used as the method of 'disposal', because that is what it is.

The Dangerous Patient

Inadequates are social nuisances and misfits ignored or even partly tolerated by society, but the dangerous patient poses inescapable problems. Because safe custody is the prime consideration, treatment is relegated to a secondary role, with fundamental contradictions in the functions of the special hospitals like Broadmoor. A detailed examination of these issues is not possible here, but a few aspects are relevant to the general topic of the abuse of psychiatry and the specific Russian problem.

In dealing with the dangerous patient public confidence must be maintained lest harshly repressive measures are imposed by a panic-stricken electorate. Of the many misunderstandings about the dangerous patient not the least is the failure to appreciate that the public can never enjoy total impregnable protection.

It is not easy to define the dangerous individual but it generally means someone likely to cause serious physical injury or lasting psychological harm. The propensity to be violent is also bound up with the situation in which the offender finds himself. Drink often has a disinhibiting effect, and sexual encounters may also influence the likelihood of a violent act. In some situations, violence is not only socially acceptable but encouraged, as in war. Some forms of sport, overtly as in boxing or covertly as in football, involve violent behaviour, not only in the participants but also in the spectators.

The relationship between violent behaviour and mental illness is complex. The majority of mentally ill patients are not violent either to others or to themselves. Even those who express violent intentions rarely give vent to them when cared for by experienced nurses. Treatment of the mental illness will lessen the likelihood of violence in any patients so predisposed. Conversely those who commit violent crimes, even repeatedly, are not necessarily mentally ill. It is no help to society to label all such criminals mad.

When a mentally ill person commits a violent act, it does not necessarily follow that the illness and the crime are connected. The forensic psychiatrist must carefully weigh up all the evidence, legal and medical. The mental disorder may have contributed to the violent act, but it is not easy to draw clear connections between a continuing morbid state of mind and an isolated, albeit extreme, act.

The public demands that the dangerous patient should

remain locked up until he no longer constitutes a danger. Where the violent behaviour is a direct consequence of some form of mental illness, recovery from the illness ensures that the violent behaviour will not recur. For example, a deeply depressed man may attempt to kill his family to save them from an imaginary dreadful fate. With his return to his normal mood the risk to the family disappears. The psychiatrist has to be allowed by the public to exercise his judgement if natural justice is to be done. If in the opinion of the courts a violent act was a direct consequence of a mental illness and that illness responds completely to treatment, it is unjust and unreasonable for the public to object to the patient's release because he has not spent 'enough' time locked up in punishment.

Where the connection between the mental illness and the violent act is more equivocal, the psychiatrist is faced with a very uncomfortable decision. It is notoriously difficult to predict whether a person who has committed a violent criminal act will repeat his offence. The basic dilemma facing the psychiatrist is how many offenders who are no longer dangerous must remain in special hospitals in order to protect the public from the unknown one among them who represents a threat. The system is biased towards retention of patients rather than premature release; often people stay locked up longer than they would if they had committed the same offence and no mental disorder had been established.

Psychiatry is in a vulnerable position in this context. Laypeople interpret the performance of a violent act by a mentally disordered individual as a cause-and-effect relationship, the corollary being that the offender is dangerous until his mental disorder has been cured. The shortcomings of psychiatry, its inability either to establish the 'real' relationship between act and mental state or to 'cure' the abnormal mental state, mean that it cannot defend itself against exploitation by society as a convenient 'disposal' for mentally ill offenders nor defend its patients against long periods of incarceration.

The Schizophrenic Patient

The treatment of the schizophrenic patient involves to a greater or lesser extent all the topics we have touched on so far – the amelioration of emotional and intellectual symptoms, the rehabilitation of the socially handicapped, and on occasion the custody of the dangerous patient. Moreover, because the available drug treatments have unpleasant side-effects we encounter similar ethical problems to those met in hormone therapy for sexual deviants, but here they are complicated by the difficulties of ensuring that consent to treatment is valid in a patient who in lay terms is mad.

The major tranquillizers are drugs which calm the disturbed patient and control many of the schizophrenic patient's symptoms. The first major tranquillizer, a phenothiazine called chlorpromazine, was introduced in 1953, its trade name in Europe being Largactil. In the U.S.A. it is called Thorazine and in the U.S.S.R. Aminazin. In an emergency, these drugs can be injected into a muscle, but this can be painful; tablets by mouth are standard treatment. Other major tranquillizers can be injected as a special long-acting preparation once every two to four weeks. This form of maintenance therapy has substantially improved the outlook for the chronic schizophrenic patient.

Side-effects are numerous (see also p. 157). All major tranquillizers can induce neurological complications such as parkinsonism (stiffness and trembling) and akathisia, in which the patient cannot keep still. The most worrying side-effects of the major tranquillizers are disabilities which only come on after several years' treatment. The best-documented is 'dyskinesia', which comprises repetitive tic-like movements of the mouth and tongue. Unlike most other side-effects, dyskinesia does not usually disappear when the drugs are discontinued; it may even get worse. Estimates of the incidence of this condition in patients taking long-term major tranquillizers range up to thirty per cent and have led to a reappraisal of the whole value of these drugs in chronically ill patients. In the United States suits for damages have been filed on behalf of patients so disabled.

With schizophrenia, both the therapeutic actions and the side-effects of drug treatment are powerful, and together with the difficulties of informed consent they throw the ethical problems into sharp relief. Where the diagnosis itself is open to dispute, the ethical considerations multiply even further because of the particular properties of the major tranquillizers. Schizophrenic patients usually tolerate large amounts of major tranquillizers; normal individuals cannot. A dose of chlorpromazine sufficient to tranquillize a disturbed schizophrenic patient without any untoward side-effects renders a normal subject overwhelmingly drowsy, faint and dry-mouthed. Continuing high doses in the normal individual induce neurological complications, dystonia and parkinsonism, which persist until the drug is discontinued. The individual is zombie-like, befuddled in mind and distressed in body.

To recapitulate, the psychiatrist is on the horns of an ethical dilemma when he diagnoses and treats a patient he has labelled 'schizophrenic'. If the diagnosis is unequivocal, the patient displays thought disorder, bizarre delusions etc. which may render him incapable of fully understanding the implications of treatment, but response may be gratifying. If the patient is minimally disturbed, he is capable of informed consent but is not as likely to derive sufficient benefit from the drug treatment to counterbalance the side-effects.

Earlier in this chapter the accidental discovery of the physical methods of treatment, insulin coma and electro-convulsive therapy (ECT), was mentioned, together with the controversial advocacy of such measures in the management of schizophrenic patients. Some quotations from standard texts will serve to highlight this important point.

One standard textbook on physical treatments (Sargant and Slater) contains the following statement (p. 24):

... we believe it is wise to give most early schizophrenics the bene-fit of a full course of ECT while under the influence of pheno-thiazines ...

Similarly with insulin coma; the authoritative *American Handbook of Psychiatry* (Vol. 5, p. 528) avers:

Insulin coma therapy must be considered a useful form of treat-ment which has helped many schizophrenic patients.

This is denied by Sim in his large textbook (p. 977):

... most psychiatrists feel, with justification, that they can obtain better results in schizophrenia without it [insulin coma therapy].

Within the covers of one multi-author book devoted to schizophrenia (Bellak and Loeb; p. 571) we find:

... the advantages of insulin coma therapy are becoming even more clearly recognized in many countries ...

– not apparently, however, by another two authorities in the preceding chapter (p. 498):

Although ECT and insulin coma treatments have been widely used, their efficacy in the treatment of schizophrenia has not been clearly established ...

One could fill pages with a chiaroscuro of such contra-dictory quotations about drugs and physical treatments; and the controversy over psychoanalysis and psychotherapy would fill volumes. But it is not the rights and wrongs of the dis-agreements which concern us but the ethical implications of recognizing that widely dissenting opinions exist. Patients need some form of protection against extreme views, even those held with sincere conviction. In particular, those under forced custody or who are mentally disabled because of their illness deserve protection from the ministrations of well-meaning but over-enthusiastic practitioners. Equally, they deserve pro-tection from well-meaning but *under*-enthusiastic psychia-trists. That protection lies in open decision-making involving patient, family, doctors, nurses and ancillary members of the therapeutic team.

Meanwhile, can more positive steps be taken to protect the public from the zealous claims of our therapeutic braggadocios? Perhaps one could establish whether a given treatment for a particular indication is recognized by a majority of practising psychiatrists or not. Such a survey with respect to barbiturates, carried out by the Research Committee of the Royal College of Psychiatrists, showed that these drugs had fallen into general disfavour but a substantial minority still used them occasionally in specific conditions such as severe panic attacks. By careful sounding out of opinion it would become apparent which treatments were recommended by most psychiatrists, or at least by an appreciable minority, and which were advocated by very few. With this information the profession could regulate itself by establishing advisory panels which the patient or his family could consult when being urged to consider a controversial treatment, especially an irreversible measure like leucotomy.

Of course such a proposal will engender howls of derision about 'therapy by committee', yelps of indignation about 'interference with clinical liberty' and cries of anguish about 'diluting the patient–doctor relationship'. But already the major centres undertaking leucotomy subject the patient to detailed assessments, and the decision whether to operate is taken jointly by the unit team. There is already interference with clinical freedom: for example, in order to limit an incipient epidemic of heroin addiction in the U.K. in the 1960s, the right to prescribe narcotics to addicts was limited to a few experienced responsible practitioners. And there is nothing more likely to dissolve the patient–doctor relationship than an unnecessary and disastrous therapeutic venture.

The unassuming psychiatrist discards the paternalistic stance of 'the doctor knows best'. Psychiatric conditions are much easier to manage with all of the patient's cooperation and that of his family. By trusting the patient and keeping him informed of the advantages, drawbacks and limitations of the proposed treatment, the psychiatrist can avoid the discomforts of a God-like pose.

The Hyperactive Child

The condition known as 'hyperactive syndrome' also exemplifies the type of abuse of psychiatric treatment that can arise when, as so often, a psychiatric diagnosis is not based on known pathology. The term denotes a pattern of behaviour more common in boys, beginning early in life and characterized by four cardinal symptoms: overactivity, impulsiveness, distractability and excitability. It is not a clear-cut condition, as it merges in its more severe forms with children with definite brain damage and in its milder forms with normality.

There is no evidence that treatment of any type significantly affects the long-term outcome for the hyperactive child, who is likely to grow up showing anti-social behaviour, academic backwardness and perhaps depression and alcoholism. Stimulant drugs like the amphetamines and methylphenidate (Ritalin) are often effective symptomatically in lessening the social and educational disabilities of the hyperactive child, but only some children respond and most still require remedial education. Other children may actually be made worse by stimulants. Furthermore, the continued administration of these drugs has been suspected of causing the suppression of growth hormone secretion and of appetite, which would culminate in stunted growth. As in the treatment of schizophrenia, long-term medication is not something to be embarked on lightly.

As there is no clear boundary between normality and hyperactivity, psychiatry is again vulnerable. It is a matter of opinion whether a high-spirited, mischievous, restless rapscallion of a boy is to be labelled 'hyperactive syndrome', thereby converting a behavioural and educational problem into a medical one. It is then an easy step to treat him with Ritalin in an attempt to lessen his boisterousness and disruptive effects in class. There were newspaper reports of large numbers of children in Omaha in the United States receiving stimulant drugs apparently without adequate medical indications or supervision. Teachers were allegedly refusing to allow some children into class unless they were dosed with medicine to quieten them. Although this obvious abuse was rectified, the basic problem still exists. Where a condition merges with normality, where no objective criteria for abnormality can be established, where treatments are powerful and have drawbacks, where treatment can be foisted on the patient, even the well-intentioned psychiatrist can find himself accused of abuse of psychiatry, of not acting in his patient's best interests.

The Ethics of Compulsion

These basic questions must be posed: 'Has society the right to force treatment on mentally ill individuals, either for their own benefit or for its own protection?'

'Should society allow psychiatrists to incarcerate individuals compulsorily?'

'Has society more rights in this respect when an offence has been committed? Does the psychiatrist serve the patient or society or both? If both, how does he maintain an ethical balance?'

Compulsory detention

The loudest voice urging that psychiatrists should not have the right to compulsory detention of their patients belongs to Thomas Szasz, Professor of Psychiatry at the State University of New York at Syracuse. Most of his arguments have some limited cogency, but it is the insistent stridency with which he repeats them that has given them widespread currency.

Szasz's trenchant criticism is that psychiatry, as practised in mental hospitals, is a social organization which strives to discharge its official duties and to extend its own power and rewards. Szasz states baldly: 'Traditionally, psychiatric hospitals have been jails.' Psychiatrists are entrusted by society through its laws with the duty to apprehend, confine and then to diagnose and treat persons regarded as mentally ill. Unlike medical admission to hospital psychiatric admission does not require the patient's consent. Thus, a person may on religious grounds refuse a blood transfusion even if it is life-saving. By contrast, hospitalization and often treatment can be forced on the psychiatric patient.

Two justifications for this are used. First, that the patient misjudges his own needs or is unaware of his unusual behaviour; secondly, that the patient must be restrained to protect those around him. Szasz regards the first point as wholly untenable; he argues idealistically that people are the best judge of their own interests. The second justification, protection of the public, is also dismissed by Szasz: 'following in the libertarian tradition, I hold that a person should be deprived of his liberty only if he is proved guilty of breaking the law.'

The key to Szasz's facile espousal of psychiatric anarchy lies in his admission that he sees patients only in an office practice; that is, people come to him with their psychiatric problems. Consequently he does not encounter the seriously ill patients who pose the real ethical and moral problems. For example, a woman may be increasingly depressed and hopeless; she may develop delusions that a horrible fate awaits her children, and to spare them that outcome she may consider killing them, and afterwards committing suicide. Or a man may become morbidly jealous of his wife, develop delusions about her supposed infidelities, and threaten to murder her. These are not hypothetical instances, as every psychiatrist in hospital practice knows. Calamities where mental illness remained unsuspected or the threats were ignored occur quite frequently in homicide records. If these patients are compulsorily admitted to hospital and treated adequately, their illnesses remit and their normal affectionate relationships are re-established. If Szasz were responsible for a potentially

69

homicidal or suicidal patient who refused voluntary admission, would he really stand by his libertarian principles and wait for the tragedy?

In fact, almost everyone who can make an informed appraisal of the dilemmas concerning the seriously mentally ill recognizes the need for legally sanctioned involuntary admission. This does not blunt Szasz's secondary criticism that such powers are being used excessively in the United States and elsewhere. This abuse partly reflects the unsavoury nature of some State mental hospitals, and it also stems from the authoritarian attitude of some psychiatrists. Szasz claims that ninety per cent of patients in public mental institutions in the U.S.A. are there involuntarily. This figure, however, covers both those formally committed and those who Szasz claims would be formally committed if they tried to leave hospital. Clearly, if these allegations contain elements of truth, closer and more strict public scrutiny is required. Mental institutions in the U.S.A. vary greatly in their standards, both medically and ethically, and some State systems urgently need review.

Nor have British psychiatrists escaped similar censure. The 1959 Mental Health Act was formulated to allow psychiatric patients to be treated like other medical patients wherever possible, but legal powers of forcible restraint and admission to mental hospital were retained.

In a Special Report of the National Association for Mental Health, Larry Gostin points out various deficiencies in the provisions and in the operation of the Act. Although some of the evidence supporting the criticisms derives from American studies of doubtful relevance to the U.K., the Report exemplifies the disquiet of many people about psychiatrists' powers. Gostin points out that it is dangerous to rely on psychiatric diagnosis, because it is a notoriously unreliable procedure. This is true but irrelevant, since compulsory admission to mental hospital depends on the behaviour of the patient, irrespective of formal diagnosis.

Nevertheless, the charge that British psychiatrists have recourse too often to compulsory admission must be taken seriously. Only one in eight of patients admitted to British mental hospitals in 1974 was under legal orders, but some others entering hospital 'voluntarily' are led to believe that compulsion would be resorted to if they were uncooperative. Mental Health Review Tribunals act as watchdogs over the psychiatric services, but Gostin shows that these Tribunals are difficult for patients to activate.

Although some psychiatrists absolutely deny any abuse of the Mental Health Act's provisions, justice must be seen to be done. The proposals for reform and for strengthening independent tribunals and assessors must not be peremptorily dismissed; they should be debated publicly and honestly as part of the check and countercheck of the democratic process.

Compulsory treatment

The usual recommendation is that mentally ill individuals should be persuaded to overcome any objections to treatment. It is assumed that those objections are the product of ignorance or prejudice or that they arise because the patient's judgement or decisiveness are impaired by his illness, or because he lacks insight into the seriousness of his condition. But it is too facile for the psychiatrist to dismiss objections to treatment as being an integral part of the illness without permitting the patient to voice his reservations to others, both within and outside the therapeutic team. Where basic human rights are being infringed, even in the apparent best interests of the patient, this unfortunate circumstance must be recognized frankly. Even where the mentally ill or handicapped are obviously in danger of neglect or exploitation, the psychiatrist's intervention must be as open as practicable. The relatives can help greatly, but they sometimes prove as reluctant as the patient to agree to the recommended treatment.

As stressed earlier, where the proposed treatment is not controversial, hazardous or irreversible, compulsion is justifiable to prevent the patient behaving violently or being a

71

danger to himself or to others, to save his life or to prevent him from deteriorating. If the treatment does represent some hazard, compulsion is ethical only where the danger has been fully explained. The patient should not be led to believe that his only hope of discharge from hospital lies specifically in the proposed treatment. If the patient cannot fully comprehend the implications of a proposed therapy, his relatives should be given a full explanation. A further ethical safeguard is for the patient or his family to have free access to a genuinely independent second opinion when either he or they object to the treatment.

This procedure should certainly be invoked where irreversible procedures such as leucotomy are contemplated. Only in this way could the public reassure themselves that doctors, even with the best intentions, are not abusing their privileged position of trust in their enthusiasm to treat a disorder. It matters little whether the doctor has powers to compulsorily treat the patient or not. Abuse produces the same end-state for the patient whether he is persuaded to undergo a treatment by an uncritical and over-enthusiastic psychiatrist or forced to undergo it because of legal powers conferred on that psychiatrist.

Conclusions

We have ranged widely but selectively over some of the ethical issues involved in 'psychiatric treatment'. Too often this term hides imprecise estimates of illness and empirically derived drugs and procedures. Many are controversial, at least for some indications, and others are really custodial rather than therapeutic. By overselling the effectiveness of many therapies, some psychiatrists have done a disservice to both themselves and their patients.

Expectations are also unrealistic among society in general, which delegates responsibility to the psychiatrist to deal not only with those coming to him with symptoms but those whose behaviour lies outside tolerated bounds. Most psychiatrists recognize the limitations of their specialty and refuse to assume unrealistic targets for treatment and rehabilitation. They balance the needs of their patients against the requirements of society, and they are hampered when society makes excessive demands.

CHAPTER 6

Psychiatry and the Law

We now start to examine more of the wider implications of psychiatry, the areas where psychiatry impinges on the theory and practice of law. Immediately we shall become aware of divergences in attitudes and practice both from country to country and in any one country over recent decades.

Scientific subjects are fairly uniform and homogeneous throughout the world except where sociological factors are important. Medicine also tends to vary only in those aspects that are determined by social, political and economic circumstances, and not in the basic scientific areas. Psychiatry is less consistent, as we have seen in our survey of diagnostic criteria for schizophrenia. Since legal practice reflects public attitudes and mores, which differ from country to country, a wide variety of laws has developed throughout the world. The relationships between components of society – authority, psychiatrists and patient/offenders – are formalized in the laws governing the medical and legal treatment of the mentally ill offender.

Not only does this area of forensic psychiatry differ from one legal system to another; often the current position can only be understood by following historical developments over past centuries. Essentially, psychiatry and the law have to contend with a morass of legal, medical, ethical and moral issues. These can be reduced to the old 'mad-or-bad' dilemma but only at the risk of over-simplifying the problem and compounding the fundamental misunderstandings between psychiatrists and jurists. The basic differences in theory and practice between the attempted precision of the law and the undoubted inexactitudes of psychiatry led to many fruitless debates. These were largely resolved when the interests of the patient/offender were given greater consideration by the law, which satisfied itself with less precision but more flexibility and humanity. In parallel, psychiatrists concerned themselves less with moral and philosophical problems of free-will and responsibility and more with practical suggestions for management and therapy.

In this chapter I have adopted a historical approach, outlining theory and practice in the United Kingdom, the United States and Soviet Russia. I have concentrated on the crime of murder, which has always provided the critical tests of any ethical, moral and medical attitudes to the mentally ill offender. Several legal concepts, including 'responsibility' and 'fitness to plead', are crucial to an understanding of the dilemmas of psychiatry. Many of the arguments are complex and even technical, but I hope the reader will appreciate the need to understand the situation in the U.K. and the U.S.A., since it is only against this background that the very different situation in the U.S.S.R. can be set in proper perspective.

Many aspects of this complex area were touched on in earlier chapters. But the problems of psychiatry are seen most openly when the psychiatrist presents a report or is cross-examined in court. Here, above all, an overstatement of the powers of psychiatry to detect abnormal mental phenomena, make firm diagnoses and provide effective treatment can result in public incredulity, disbelief and discredit.

Historical

In the barbarous Middle Ages, religious intolerance governed public attitudes to many people who undoubtedly were mentally disturbed. The clerical authorities attributed mad behaviour to possession by demons. Some unfortunate women were accused of witchcraft and of consorting with the devil.

The *Malleus Maleficarum* ('The Hammer of Witchcraft'), which Jacobus Sprenger and Heinrich Kramer wrote in 1486 as the witch-catcher's manual, states (p. 100):

... the devil can draw out some image retained in a faculty corresponding to one of the senses; as he draws from the memory, which is in the back part of the head, an image of a horse, and locally moves that phantasm to the middle part of the head, where are the cells of the imaginative power; and finally to the sense of reason, which is in the front of the head. And he causes such a sudden change and confusion that such objects are necessarily thought to be actual things seen with the eyes. This can be clearly exemplified by the natural defect in frantic men and other maniacs.

This describes hallucinations. (Speculation about the mechanisms of the brain is much the same today, except that the devil is not usually invoked.)

A horrible death awaited the wretched 'witches'; in 1515 500 people were executed in Geneva in three months. The more fortunate madman deemed to be possessed by a demon would be exorcized, which proved as unsuccessful in deluded patients then as it was in a recent tragic case in the North of England.

Belief in witchcraft is now officially discredited in developed countries, but it lingers covertly in folk-lore. Belief in demoniac possession is still extant in more conservative ecclesiastical circles.

The Age of Reason in Europe was accompanied by custodial treatment, often in brutal conditions, of those bereft of reason. As contemporary accounts and drawings depict, the mad were derided, the Sunday afternoon outing to Bethlem providing fashionable entertainment.

At the beginning of the nineteenth century, Pinel, a French psychiatrist, unchained the inmates of the Bicêtre Mental Hospital in Paris – the first step towards substituting sympathetic treatment for custodial care. There is still far to go and the rate of progress hangs on shifts in public opinion.

In parallel with the slow reform of the management of the mad, attempts were made to liberalize the treatment of the bad; both movements reflected the more intense humanitarian sentiments exemplified in the abolition of slavery. Nineteenth-century judges found themselves dispensing savage penalties introduced in the preceding century in an attempt to counter the crime wave that followed on industrialization and urbanization. Mitigating circumstances or legal loopholes were increasingly used to avoid the mandatory death sentence for minor offences, or, more commonly, juries refused to convict.

Crimes can be divided into two types, those with strict liability and those requiring criminal intent. An example of a strict liability crime is driving a motor vehicle with a concentration of alcohol in the blood in excess of 80 mg per 100 ml. Even if the accused did not mean to have an excessive alcohol intake, provided that the technical requirements such as proper administration of the breathalyser have been met, he will be found guilty, convicted and given a sentence, including the mandatory disqualification. In the other type of crime the state of mind of the accused is paramount. Here, the legal premise is that it is unjust to punish people for their acts because the illegal act might turn out to have been accidental. Traditionally the law attached great importance to the purpose of the accused, criminal intentions being necessary. The concept of criminal intent evolved greatly during the nineteenth century and the present century.

To establish criminal intent the court decides on the state of mind of the accused as he committed the crime. However, states of mind of apparently normal people are not easily determined. A barren controversy has smouldered on between psychiatry and the law (to be accurate, between some psychiatrists and some lawyers), mainly because each profession has argued from different viewpoints with mutual misunderstandings. In particular, psychiatrists have failed to comprehend that the law makes decisions, and lawyers have been impatient with ambiguous psychiatric formulations.

The Law in Britain

In the following sections the legal situation in the British Isles, the U.S.A. and Soviet Russia is outlined. However, one can only begin to understand the legal and psychiatric philosophies underlying current practice in the context of its historical development. For that reason the procedures in England are relevant to American practice, since the American legal system developed from the English, and moreover, for decades after Independence, the American judiciary was influenced by English court decisions. As will be seen, the Soviets differ in practice and fundamental attitudes from both British and American systems, being concerned to educate the public as well as to punish the miscreant.

The Law in England and Wales

CRIMINAL RESPONSIBILITY AND MURDER. Murder has always been the crime of most concern to the general public. As it is in many ways atypical, the principles underlying legal processes concerning murder are not automatically applicable to lesser crimes.

The problem of responsibility for murder has vexed the psychiatric and legal professions for over a century. Public interest was aroused in 1843 when Daniel McNaughton, a Glasgow wood-turner, was tried for the wilful murder of Edward Drummond, private secretary to Sir Robert Peel. McNaughton, mistaking Drummond for the Prime Minister, shot him before numerous witnesses, including a police constable. McNaughton was a paranoid schizophrenic with long-standing delusions of persecution directed in particular at the 'Tories'. The medical witnesses concurred that the accused was too insane to exercise self-control. The judge stopped the trial and the jury returned a verdict of 'not guilty by reason of insanity'. McNaughton was acquitted but committed to Bethlem, where he remained for many years until he was transferred to the Criminal Lunatic Asylum, Broadmoor, soon after it opened.

Note the 'not guilty' verdict. Although McNaughton was apparently acting unlawfully, there was no evidence of intent: McNaughton was not to be blamed; he was not culpable, not accountable and not responsible. Because 'not guilty', Mc-Naughton was formally acquitted, but he was nevertheless incarcerated in a mental hospital.

The public were so incensed by the verdict that an ancient but rarely used procedure was activated. The judges as a body were summoned to the House of Lords and requested to formulate the existing state of the law with respect to insanity. One wise judge demurred at interpreting the theory of the law in isolation from an actual case, but the others enumerated three propositions, later to be called the Mc-Naughton Rules:

1. Every man is presumed to be sane and to possess a sufficient degree of reason to be responsible until the contrary is proved.

2. To establish a defence on the ground of insanity, it must be clearly proved that, at the time of committing the act, the party accused was labouring under such a defect of reason, from disease of the mind, as not to know the nature and quality of the act he was doing, or if he did know it, that he did not know he was doing what was wrong.

3. If he is under an insane delusion and commits an offence in consequence thereof, he must be considered in the same situation as to responsibility as if the facts with respect to which the delusion exists were real.

Rule 1 is unexceptionable. Rule 2 poses almost impossible questions about whether the accused knew the nature and quality of the act, knew that what he did was wrong, and so on. Most severely mentally retarded patients would fit clearly into this category, but few mentally ill patients are so mad that they are unaware of their actions. 'Knowledge' is not a mental faculty greatly affected in mental illness; perception, emotion and the will are more significant areas. Rule 2 is inconsistent with the outcome of McNaughton's case; if the judge had applied it, McNaughton would probably have been convicted, as he knew what he was doing and that it was wrong, but his delusions were too forceful for him to resist. Rule 3 illustrates the *reductio ad absurdum* of lawyers' logic when they have no actual case before them to exercise their acumen.

The McNaughton Rules quickly became a legal straitjacket preventing flexibility, although many judges stretched them almost to breaking in order to be merciful. Psychiatric evidence was constrained within the framework of the rules, judges varied in their application of the rules, and the impossibly strict criteria disadvantaged the mentally sick.

Because murder and madness are emotive topics, law reform was hindered, and as late as 1922 a committee of the Lord Chancellor reaffirmed the McNaughton Rules. The Scots, however, with their customary legal common sense, ignored the Rules and modified the law in step with advances in psychiatric knowledge. As long ago as 1867, Lord Deas introduced in Scotland the concept of diminished responsibility, which proved practicable.

Ninety years later, the Homicide Act of 1957 introduced into England the defence of diminished responsibility, which reduces the charge of murder to one of manslaughter. Diminished responsibility is defined as follows:

Where a person kills or is party to the killing of another, he shall not be convicted of murder if he was suffering from such abnormality of mind (whether arising from a condition of arrested or retarded development of mind or any inherent causes or induced by disease or injury) as substantially impaired his mental responsibility for his acts and omissions in doing or being a party to the killing.

The very imprecision of the formulation – the difficulty of defining 'substantially' or 'mental responsibility' or, particularly, 'inherent causes' – is its strength, allowing the courts adequate flexibility to procedure and sentencing. In 1973 nearly a quarter of those indicted for murder were convicted of the lesser charge of manslaughter following the defence of diminished responsibility. Each year one or two people accused of murder fall within the McNaughton Rules, the verdict being 'not guilty by reason of insanity'.

UNFIT TO PLEAD. A fundamental principle of English law is that no man should be tried unless his mental condition is such that he can defend himself. Counsel for a person charged with an indictable offence in a higher court may submit that his client is unfit to plead at the beginning of the trial, on arraignment, or at any point during the trial. A special jury decides whether the prisoner is fit to plead by considering the following criteria:

The accused should be mentally capable of
1. Instructing his legal advisers, in particular, counsel.
2. Appreciating the significance of pleading 'guilty' or 'not guilty'.
3. Challenging a juror.
4. Examining (questioning) witnesses.
5. Understanding and following the evidence and court procedure.

If the accused fails to respond when asked to plead 'guilty' or 'not guilty', the jury has to decide whether he is mute 'of malice' or 'by the visitation of God'. If he can communicate by reading and writing he is deemed sane and the trial proceeds. If he is declared 'mute of malice', the trial proceeds as if a plea of 'not guilty' had been entered.

Competency to plead is not the same as sanity. An accused person may be undeniably mentally ill and yet be fit to plead because he fulfils the above criteria. He may then be found to have diminished responsibility. Thus insanity, responsibility at the time of the crime, and competency to plead at the time of the trial are *separate* legal concepts.

Most accused found unfit to plead are mentally subnormal; but schizophrenic, manic and paranoid patients may also qualify. Usually a medical report has been prepared while the accused was in custody.

In 1956, before the reforming Homicide Act, eighteen per cent of persons indicted for murder were found unfit to plead; in 1973 only one per cent fell into this category. The defence of diminished responsibility is considered a more satisfactory mode of justice, for one reason in particular. If the accused is deemed unfit to plead, the case is not immediately closed but 'lies on the lists' for some time. In fact, the accused is committed, usually to Broadmoor, 'until Her Majesty's pleasure shall become known'. If competency to plead is regained he can in theory be tried, but in practice this is rare. The greatest injustice is that the facts of the case may never be tried, so that the accused could be sent to a mental hospital for a crime he did not commit. With the defence of diminished responsibility for murder and with the treatment provisions of the Mental Health Act, 1959, for lesser offences, justice is dispensed and the most appropriate treatment given. Of course, the accused may have been sane at the time of the crime and become unfit to plead only later. The diminished responsibility mechanism is then obviously inapplicable.

There are some interesting implications of the manoeuvre of 'unfit to plead'. A manifestly insane accused person may be so devoid of insight as to deny any mental illness. A severely depressed man may be so saturated with guilt and despair that he willingly accepts any penalty. In these instances counsel may make the claim that his client is unfit to plead against the express instructions of his client. Naturally, counsel would do this reluctantly, but he has a responsibility to the court and the interests of justice. Medical evidence would be produced to support the submission of unfitness to plead.

Nevertheless, an appeal procedure is vital. In practice, it uses the machinery of the Court of Appeal under the Criminal Procedure (Insanity) Act, 1964. If the appeal is allowed, the accused may then be tried for the offence for which he was charged. The Court of Appeal may also allow an appeal against the finding of unfitness to plead if it is of the 'opinion that the case is one in which the accused should have been acquitted before the question of fitness to be tried was considered.' Thus the Court can both quash the finding of un-fitness to plead and direct a verdict of acquittal to be re-corded.

Although by no means perfect, the system has definite safe-guards for the accused if an 'unfit to plead' claim is made. A jury (and to a great extent the judge who directs them) deliberates on the evidence presented, and the patient and his relatives have a right of appeal. Nevertheless, reluctance to invoke the expedient is reflected by its declining use.

The Law in Scotland

In Scotland, controversies over the interpretation of the Mc-Naughton Rules were obviated because of the long-standing use of the concept of diminished responsibility in relation to murder (see p. 80). The Mental Health Act (1960), Scot-land, set up an independent Mental Welfare Board with five to seven commissioners, two of whom are medical. It is respon-sible for general supervision of the mentally disabled and has wide powers, including the functions discharged in England and Wales by the Mental Health Review Tribunals.

The Law in the United States

The McNaughton Rules were adopted throughout the English-speaking world, including the U.S.A. But the disenchantment with the Rules was expressed by Sobeloff, with typical Ameri-can forthrightness: 'Why should we maintain a Rule that must be breached in order to make it work?'

An early circumvention of the Rules occurred in 1886, when a decision in the Alabama Supreme Court accepted 'irresist-ible impulse' as a valid defence. This stratagem has been used in a few cases since then, but objections to it are strong. An irresistible impulse has been ridiculed as an impulse which has not been resisted. Establishing the existence of such an impulse at the time of the criminal act is very difficult, especially if the impulse is viewed as an isolated element of the accused's mental state. From the medical point of view such impulses usually occur in brain conditions such as epilepsy or encephalitis (brain inflammation) which produce other obvious signs of illness, so that the concept of irresistible impulse becomes superfluous.

In the U.S.A., only the New Hampshire jurisdiction opted to ignore the McNaughton Rules entirely; instead it was ruled in 1871 that 'a product of mental disease is not a contract, a will or a crime'. In other words, if the unlawful act was a consequence of the mental illness, the accused could not be convicted. Ascertaining whether an individual was mentally diseased and whether his actions were a product of that illness was acknowledged to be difficult, but the problems were practical not legal.

In the Durham Case in 1954, the Court of Appeal for the District of Columbia rejected the McNaughton Rules and the irresistible impulse formulation and applied a test akin to the New Hampshire product rule. An accused was not criminally responsible if his unlawful act was the product of mental disease or mental defect. The limitations of the McNaughton Rules were superseded by a reliance on psychiatrists' evidence regarding mental disease and its relationship to the accused's actions. The Durham Rule, in turn, attracted cogent criticisms because mental disease and mental defect were not clearly defined. Since psychiatrists commonly disagree about diagnosis, the administration of the rule was inevitably uncertain and unequal. This problem was particularly apparent with psychopathic criminals, because ideas about the 'psychopath' or 'sociopath', the grossly deviant anti-social individual, are even more inchoate than those concerning schizophrenic or depressive patients. Another requirement is to establish the causal connection between the illness and the criminal act, so that it can be reasonably inferred that the accused would not have committed the crime if he had not been diseased. A link must exist between the disease and the act, and whatever its strength it must be critical and decisive in nature.

Some States adopted the product rule, despite the criticisms levelled at it. Others prevaricated, partly because of the alternative suggested by the American Law Institute, the research branch of the American Bar Association:

A person is not responsible for criminal conduct if at the time of such conduct as a result of mental disease or defect he lacks substantial capacity either to appreciate the criminality of his conduct or to conform his conduct to the requirements of law. The terms 'mental disease or defect' do not include an abnormality manifested only by repeated criminal or otherwise anti-social conduct.

The first condition, 'to appreciate the criminality of his conduct', merely rephrases the McNaughton Rule of 'did not know he was doing what was wrong', and it is subject to the same criticism of limiting mental disease to the area of 'knowing'. The alternative condition is also vague: what do 'substantial capacity' and 'conform his conduct' mean?

Nevertheless, this formulation or approximations to it are prevailing over the Durham product rule. In what was essentially a test case, the U.S. Court of Appeal for the District of Columbia in 1972 eliminated the Durham rule and considered an individual as not responsible for criminal conduct if 'at the time of such conduct as a result of a mental disease or defect he lacks substantial capacity to appreciate the wrongfulness of his conduct or to conform his conduct to the requirements of the law'. Mental disease or defect was held to include 'any abnormal condition of the mind which substantially affects mental or emotional processes and substantially affects behavior controls'.

This type of theoretical formulation conceptualizes responsibility in all-or-nothing terms and lacks the pragmatic flexibility of the English quantitative system of diminished responsibility. In practice, however, American courts are capable of flexible and humane treatment of the mentally disturbed, although the exercise of this capacity varies from State to State. The increase in crime in the U.S.A. has hardened attitudes to the use of insanity as a defence, especially as this defence has been entered in cases in which it was not readily apparent or appropriate.

Unfit to plead

The criteria whether an accused is fit to plead are the same in the U.S.A. as in the U.K. In the U.K., special hospitals (Broadmoor, Rampton, Moss Side and Park Lane) are available for such patients, and despite their appalling problems these hospitals profess a treatment orientation. The situation in the U.S.A. is often more unsatisfactory, with patients being immured in the maximum security sections of huge mental hospitals. Patients confined in these mental hospitals because of incompetency to stand trial far outnumber those found not guilty by reason of insanity. A third group comprises convicts who develop mental illnesses while in prison and are transferred to security wings of mental hospitals, where they used to remain for years after the expiry of their original sentences. Over half of those found unfit to plead spent the rest of their lives in hospital. Many State mental hospitals in the U.S.A. are overcrowded, understaffed and orientated to custodial rather than active treatment care. The back wards of some of the hospitals in the U.S.A. which I have visited discredit such a rich country.

Most States in the U.S.A. have statutory provision for a patient to appeal against commitment to a mental hospital. Under the Constitution of the United States, all persons including patients have the right to petition for a writ of *habeas corpus*, that is to appear in court for their case to be re-examined. Because of the legal complexities this right is not often exercised, but many States now have specific legislation to define the rights of the mentally ill. Thus the patient can be visited by a legal representative, a clergyman, physician or friend of his choice. Censorship of mail is prohibited, and the patient has a right to privacy, to wear his own clothing, to retain his own money and property and to supervise his business affairs. The patient's consent to his treatment must be informed, that is, it must be explained to him, the potential advantages weighed against the possible drawbacks.

Such assertion of rights for the insane might be thought inapposite. In fact, very few psychiatric patients are lacking in all sense. They usually function competently in most spheres of mental life, showing abnormalities only in particular areas such as those relating to their delusions or morbid fears.

American psychiatrists and jurists are not complacent about the possible miscarriage of justice which may follow a finding of incompetency to stand trial. Suggestions have been made that a person found unfit to plead should be confined to hospital for a finite and limited period of time, say six months, and be treated adequately. Should competence to plead be regained, he would return to court to stand trial. If still unfit to plead the patient would be treated for a further six months and then reassessed. If still incompetent, the criminal charges would be dropped and the patient committed to hospital using civil procedures. A dangerous patient would remain confined but his case would be reviewed regularly.

The Law in the Soviet Union

Soviet law has much in common with the legal system of the West, but there are differences in emphasis, attitudes and purpose. Legal codes stem from the political, economic and cultural systems of the country, and even before the Revolution Russian law was nationally characteristic.

Conceptions in Soviet law hark back to the Russian Orthodox Church's views on the corporate character of sin. Criminals were reckoned to be unfortunate victims of society or of their own human shortcomings. They were pitiable and the community shared the burden of guilt. This view is *antilegal*, for if the criminal is merely an unfortunate there is no moral justification for prosecuting him and no logic in punishing him. Nevertheless, the Russian peasant felt acutely that the community must be protected against those jeopardizing its integrity. Many Russians wavered ambivalently between acknowledging the *political* necessity of protecting society and the state against potential disruption and tempering the punishment of the *individual* offender with charitable forgiveness.

The Russian legal system embodied a concern for the mentality of the criminal, his psychological make-up, motivation and attitudes. While it is an exaggeration to claim that the punishment was tailored to the criminal rather than the crime, it was usual for it to be related to the criminal within his social context. Of particular importance was the way in which the punishment might modify the criminal's role in society, especially his usefulness to the local community.

To this end, pre-revolutionary Russian criminal law emphasized the need to determine the state of mind of the accused at the time he allegedly committed the crime. A person was not guilty unless he acted illegally by intention or by negligence. A person must have desired the consequences (direct intent) or consciously allowed the consequences (indirect intent) or should have foreseen the consequences (negligence). The subjective state of the accused's mind closely concerned the courts.

Following the 1917 Revolution the Russian legal system was consigned to limbo. Marxist theory stipulates that laws are needed only where bourgeois and capitalist exploitation promotes excessive inequality. Law is politics; the legal system serves the interests of the ruling class as a formal enshrinement of the principles of property. A Communist revolution culminates in a classless society in which mankind is free and equal, so that a legal codex is redundant. This idealist society, devoid of prejudice, privilege, rancour or competition, comprises people living by a pure moral code of conduct. Such a utopian society would eventually abolish central powers of the state.

Lenin and the Bolsheviks despised the legalism of the West with its emphasis on property rights. With the abolition of private ownership of land and the means of production, the prohibition of private trading and of the inheritance of wealth, the direction of labour and the encouragement of moneyless transactions between state enterprises, the apparent imminence of the utopian society rendered the legal system obsolescent. The pre-revolutionary legal system was ruthlessly dismantled in an anarchic flurry. The concept of 'guilt' was suspect: Soviet criminal codes put the words 'crime' and 'punishment' in brackets after the principal phrases 'socially dangerous acts' and 'measures of social defence'. Crime was the outcome of social conflict, the criminal was to be understood and society to be defended — all pre-revolutionary ecclesiastical attitudes.

By the mid-1930s it was obvious that the Communist Millenium was some way off still and a legal system was not redundant after all. The underlying concepts also shifted, placing more stress than previously on crime and punishment. Even so, the pendulum did not swing so far that Soviet Russian practice or theory approximated to those of the West. In the Western systems the criterion for guilt relates to conduct expected of the average man, John Doe, or that traveller on the Clapham omnibus. In Russian law the criterion is 'whether under the given circumstances the given personality, with its individual capacities, development and qualifications, could have foreseen the consequences which occurred'. This subjective standard has been explicitly stated in successive criminal codes.

The crime and the criminal are set against the social context, which with major crimes and major criminals is the State. Penalties are increased for crimes which are minor transgressions of personal morality but appear dangerous to the State in the eyes of the ruling bureaucrats. Thus Soviet law may deal leniently with offences against private property or with crimes involving individuals, but it ruthlessly punishes those found guilty of crimes adversely affecting society as a whole. Murder without aggravating circumstances results in ten year's deprivation of liberty, currency speculation in the Draconian sentence of death.

From the view of crime as an outcome of a particular individual's relationship to society stems the stress on the ritual act of confession as a cleansing absolution both of the individual and of society. The mea culpas absolve the community of its guilt; in major cases, the Soviet State, purified and immaculate, can be held up once more for the adoration of the masses. Furthermore, the Soviet courts regard the sentence as educational as well as preventive. For re-education to succeed, past mistakes must be recognized, acknowledged and expiated.

To recapitulate, the Soviet system emphasizes the subjective aspects of crime as a reflection of its obsessive concern with the state of mind of the Soviet people. Criminal deviation of the individual is a special category of social deviation. For political or religious dissidence, concern is deepest and repression most thorough.

The Procuracy

One component of the Soviet judicial system quite unfamiliar to the Western lawyer is the Procuracy. The Soviet Constitution lays down that 'supreme supervisory power over the strict execution of the laws by all ministries and institutions subordinated to them, as well as by public servants and citizens of the U.S.S.R., is vested in the Procurator General of the U.S.S.R.'. The Procurator General is appointed by the Supreme Soviet for a term of seven years. He in turn appoints Procurators at lower levels. The Procuracy system purports to function independently of all local organizations, being accountable solely to the Procurator General.

Among the departments in the Procurator's Office are a Bureau of Investigation which supervises the preliminary inquiries into a case conducted by the police; a department which supervises investigations carried out by the K.G.B.; and a department for the supervision of places of confinement. The Procurator's Office has the power to order the arrest of suspected criminals, and it appoints the examining magistrates who conduct the pre-trial investigations of major crimes (like the French *juge d'instruction*). The Procurator keeps a watching brief on all criminal and civil cases and may intercede at any stage. He can 'protest' a case to a higher court, that is, formally draw its attention to a miscarriage of justice or to a sentence regarded as too lenient. The Procuracy has no administrative power of its own but sets in train the machinery of other agencies in order to activate them or to correct the errors and excesses of their subordinate branches. In a way it combines the functions of the Ombudsman, Parliamentary Select Committees and the Public Prosecutor's Office in the U.K., the Attorney General's Office, Congressional investigating committees, grand juries and public prosecutors in the U.S.A. The Procurators are also enjoined to visit and inspect at regular intervals all places of confinement within their jurisdiction, to hear complaints and to order the release of all those deemed illegally confined.

With such an admirable body, it might well be asked how the terrible excesses of Stalin were permitted and why political repression is rife even now. As in many Russian institutions the theoretical and idealistic aspects become submerged in the practical realities. The citizen has a large number of basic rights without effective means of enforcing them. The Procuracy is a state agency like the executive, legislative and judicial branches of government in the Soviet system. As the 'eye of the State', it supervises affairs *in the interests of the. State*. Furthermore, as it combines the functions of prosecutor and guardian of the accused's rights, conflicts of interest are inevitable and are almost always resolved in favour of the State. Finally, membership of the Communist Party is normally obligatory for admission to the Procuracy. Thus the power of the central authorities is unabated.

Forensic Psychiatry

As we have seen, the Soviet legal system is not concerned with what an 'average' man would have foreseen but rather with what the defendant should have anticipated in the light of his own background, capabilities and intelligence. Because the

91

Soviet procedure involves intensive pre-trial investigation of the accused by the examining magistrate or judge, much of the accused's psychological structure is uncovered. Nevertheless, this interest in the state of mind of the accused reflects not so much an idealistic solicitude for the unfortunate accused as the court's recognition of its educational role. Thus, the Soviet criminal court seeks to shape, influence and correct the thinking, attitudes and values of the criminal, and in a wider context to use him as an example to develop public standards of responsibility and behaviour vis-à-vis society and in particular the State. One is reminded of the medieval inquisitionaries searching into the hearts and minds of men to root out heresy and inculcate the current orthodoxies in the public. In the Soviet system the underlying premise is that love of country and family, respect for State property, conscientiousness and acquiescence can be instilled by the conscious decisions and actions of legislators, administrators, judges, and in particular of the Communist Party.

As an inevitable outcome of this subjectivism in Soviet law, forensic psychiatry is important, influential and wide-ranging in the system. After the Revolution questions of responsibility and competence were taken out of the hands of the courts altogether; all persons who pleaded mental illness were placed under the jurisdiction of the medical administration. Fairly soon, the criminal codes stipulated that the establishment of responsibility was the court's function, but in practice the forensic expert actually decided the question of criminal insanity, since his conclusions were almost invariably accepted by the courts. As scorn for the legal system burgeoned during the 1920s and early 1930s, forensic psychiatrists used increasingly wide criteria. The psychiatric definition of mental illness amounting to non-responsibility included all major psychiatric illness and much minor illness as well. Eventually the question of legal sanity was decided by psychiatrists in terms of the optimal treatment for that particular offender in his context in society.

In 1936 a reaction set in and forensic psychiatrists were

criticized for designating anyone with mental illness or emotional instability as legally non-responsible. With the re-establishment of the legal system and its greater emphasis on moral responsibility and freedom, the role of the forensic psychiatrist was redefined and restricted. He was to concern himself with the accused as a person and to use legal criteria for non-responsibility. In particular the needs of society were over-riding. Soviet psychiatrists have become more judicious: the percentage of accused individuals found non-responsible or unfit to plead steadily declined from the 1930s to the 1950s, at least with respect to non-political offences.

The Present Situation

Article 11 of the Fundamentals of Criminal Legislation of the U.S.S.R. states:

> A person who at the time of commission of a socially dangerous act was in a state of legal irresponsibility – that is, was unable to account for or govern his actions because of chronic mental illness, temporary mental disorder, dementia, or any other morbid state – shall not be held criminally accountable. Compulsory medical measures, established by the legislature of the Union Republics, may be applied to such a person by court order.
>
> A person who commits an offence while legally responsible but who is stricken by a mental illness that deprives him of the ability to account for or govern his actions before the court has pronounced sentence shall not be liable to punishment. Compulsory medical measures may be applied to such a person by court order according to which, after recovery, said person is again liable to punishment.

These formulas for non-accountability and unfitness to plead depend on two criteria, the medical-psychiatric one for the presence of mental illness, and the juridical-psychological for the effects of that mental illness on mental processes. The latter criterion is divided into two aspects – the intellectual, the inability to know the nature of one's actions, and the volitional, the inability to control those actions. Non-responsibility must be related to the particular socially dangerous act of which the individual is accused. There is no attempt to determine the motives of the accused. Nor need a cause-and-effect relationship between mental illnesses and the offence be established. The Soviet forensic psychiatrist verifies whether the accused was mentally ill when the offence was committed and whether the mental illness was so severe as to render him incapable of accounting for the criminal actions or of governing his behaviour during their commission.

About half the accused persons declared not responsible or unfit to plead in the Soviet Union are diagnosed as suffering from schizophrenia, and almost every individual labelled schizophrenic is deemed not responsible. Soviet forensic psychiatrists regard schizophrenic illness processes as almost inevitably impairing mental functions so that responsible acts are impossible. Indeed they emphasize that the morbid schizophrenic process indiscriminately damages all mental functions to a greater or lesser extent. Even when the psychiatrist elicits only a few morbid symptoms, his decision about the legal accountability of the patient incorporates his concept that schizophrenia changes the whole personality. The standard authorized textbook (Morozov and Kalashnik) declaims: 'Those psychiatrists and jurists are in error who attempt to cast doubt on the legal irresponsibility of schizophrenics when socially dangerous actions cannot be associated with any evident psychopathology' (p. 222). This statement negates any juridical criterion of non-responsibility and reduces the medical-psychiatric criterion to a formality. Once the forensic psychiatrist has diagnosed schizophrenia, he deems the accused non-responsible, and in practice the court concurs. If the crime was committed during a period of remission, the schizophrenic is still designated non-responsible, because Soviet forensic psychiatrists regard even prolonged and persistent remissions as nonetheless associated with personality changes (p. 225).

CHAPTER 7

The Soviet Union and Dissent

In the next chapters, we abruptly turn aside from considering general problems of psychiatry to looking in more detail at the gravest allegations made against contemporary psychiatry, its abuse in the Soviet Union. The previous chapter outlined the contrasts between Western and Soviet forensic psychiatric theory and practice. To understand these differences requires some discussion of the Russian systems of politics and economics. This I attempt in this chapter, but I do not claim an expert knowledge of these matters. I have selected certain areas of Soviet life for discussion, and I hope I shall provide the reader with some insights into Soviet Russia and perhaps in particular into the reasons for its intolerance of political and religious dissent.

Soviet Russia is different, unusual, idiosyncratic, even sometimes extraordinary, but one feels at first sight that some sort of coherent and logical system must operate, even if it is not immediately obvious. On longer acquaintance with the Soviet colossus, one realizes uneasily that either no logic exists, or a bureaucratic pandemonium prevails, or, worst, any existing logic originates from unverifiable premises. These propositions form an internally consistent system and are dangerously alluring to those social and political theorists who ignore biological determinants of human conduct such as reward.

Soviet organizations, institutions and processes differ so much from ours that the field of study must be expanded to cover many aspects of Russian life which initially seem irrelevant. For example, in the U.S.S.R. economic performance entirely reflects direct political decisions instead of being partly influenced indirectly by fiscal measures as in the West. Furthermore, reliable information is not readily released by the authorities, and when it is available language problems obtrude. For observant tourists, even experienced ones, the 'culture shock' on first visiting Russia is profound – certainly in my case more so than in any other country I have visited. On my first visit to Moscow it was immediately obvious to me that I was not in Asia; it became quickly apparent I was not really in Europe; and finally I recognized that Russia was a continent of its own.

Geographical and Historical Background

The total area of Russia is $8\frac{1}{2}$ million square miles, making it the biggest country in the world. It is nearly three times the size of the United States; the U.K. (area 94,000 square miles) would fit insignificantly into one corner. Most of Russia lies sufficiently far north to undergo climatic extremes, especially of cold. Much of Siberia has too short a summer and too long a winter to sustain agriculture. Moscow has four or five months of frost and snow each winter, being on average 13°C (24°F) colder than London, though it has about the same temperature in summer. The most equable weather is enjoyed by the areas around the Black Sea. The Caucasus has a Mediterranean-type climate, and grape-vines and citrus fruits flourish.

The Ukraine, the south-west region, is a huge, fertile granary, but most of the rest of the country is poorly endowed for agriculture. Communications within Russia are poor because of the vast distances, the infinite forests and the severe climate. Air travel has been developed as the obvious solution, and in Russia production of the supersonic plane is not for reasons of prestige but for economic utility.

The first Russian state, which grew up around Kiev, derived its civilization from the Eastern Byzantine Roman Empire of Constantinople, as witnessed by the form of Christianity of the Russian Orthodox Church. But invasion from the south-east by the Tatars disrupted this link, and Russia, now centred on Moscow, developed in isolation, culminating in 1547 in the crowning of the first Tsar. From this time on Russia expanded. An outlet to the Baltic was established and consolidated by the foundation of St Petersburg, which became the capital. Rapid movement to the east went largely unopposed by the nomadic Asiatic tribes, and the Pacific was reached by the middle of the seventeenth century. Coercion was used to colonize these vast tracts, either by forcibly settling crown serfs or by banishing prisoners, criminals and political un-desirables.

Russia was isolated by the extreme climate, by Asiatic nomads to the east, the Teutons to the west, the Swedes to the north-west and the Turks to the south. Roman civilization did not extend beyond Romania, Byzantine civilization was only in brief contact with Russia, and while the Renaissance flourished Russia was beset by enemies and the Slavs were fighting for survival. Autocratic regimes discouraged com-munication with the West or reserved such contacts for the aristocracy. Central control was absolute. The individuality of Russian institutions, systems, attitudes and values is hardly surprising.

Among the Russian people there is boundless patriotism, a sense of solidarity, of belonging not just to a large country, the centre of World Communism, but to a long historical tradition. One encounters a profound faith in the resilience and fortitude of the Russian worker, industrial or peasant, a belief well-founded in the survival of Russia in two World Wars. This patriotic fervour and trust in the ultimate destiny of the Slav nation suffer the bureaucracy to function and the government to rule. Without such intense feelings the country could not have survived its centuries of struggle and the agonies inflicted by the self-styled Master Race in the last war. Russia lost over 25 million dead; of 5 million soldiers taken prisoner, fewer than 2 million survived.

Centralism and Bureaucracy

The usual first impression of Russia is of luxuriant bureaucracy compounded by insufficient functionaries, so that all official transactions involve queuing in an orderly, British fashion. But once one fathoms the purpose of some of the obscure but obligatory transactions, circumventing official delays becomes easier and almost a pleasurable challenge. The Russians themselves apologize for their bureaucracy, but unless they are senior members of the Communist Party they are also under its exasperating control. However, Russian bureaucrats approached by the petitioner in the right way – a mixed attitude of bluster, toleration and supplication – usually help if they can. Unfortunately their duties, responsibilities and powers are not clearly defined; they are not encouraged to use any initiative, and trouble ensues if they arrogate their superiors' powers.

This bureaucratic centralism long antedates the Revolution. Because of the expansion of the Russian Empire, with its vast distances and poor communications, the danger of a centrifugal fragmentation always haunted the autocrats in power. To keep control, all administrative decisions of any importance and many trivial ones were taken centrally. Moreover, preoccupation with defence lent the administration a distinctly military flavour. The country was ruled by governors appointed centrally, who were given advice by the local gentry but were not obliged to accept it.

Marxism in Russia

Karl Marx forecast that the Communist revolution would originate in the industrialized capitalist nations of the West, such as Germany. Instead, backward, peasant-tilled Russia raised the Red Banner first. The chaos of the First World War, the opportunism of Lenin, and the pusillanimity of the opposition all contributed. The Revolution was not a complete Communist revolution but an exchange of one oligarchy for another, admittedly much more widely based; although the Russian system changed emphases, it did not alter its fundamentals. Agricultural land was confiscated from the landowners and rich peasants by the State, but agricultural efficiency still remains low. The bureaucracy adjusted to its new masters but remained ineffective because of inertia and deep conservatism. Industrialization was forced through and changed Russia into an industrialized country; but industrialization had been proceeding rapidly before the Revolution, and some countries with unchanged capitalist political and social systems have prospered at least as much.

What Marxism-Leninism really imposed was an accepted ideology, the party line. Marxism is a complete system: it claims to have the solutions to all man's political, economic and social problems. Any system adhering to these tenets should function perfectly. This belief is a dogma rather than refutable scientific theory, and it underlies many of the political and other differences between the West and Soviet Russia. If a system is theoretically perfect but has faults in practice (as the Soviet system assuredly does), it must follow that either the populace are traitors to the system – at the least not cooperating, at worst actively obstructing its functioning – or foreign saboteurs are at work: it cannot be conceded that the system has flaws. This attitude of the Soviet authorities was clearly evident in the show trials of the 1930s, when both Russians and Western technicians working in Russia fell victim to this paranoia.

In the West nobody, not even politicians, regards the system as unblemished. Failures stem from deficiencies in the organization which must be reformed, rapidly in the opinion of radicals, slowly according to the conservatives, or changed back, as viewed by the reactionaries. These fundamental differences in political outlook alienate East and West, and much of what we censure as political intolerance in the Soviets stems from their defensive attitudes towards their system.

The Communist Party

Most Russians who have responsible jobs and all those who exercise real power are members of the Communist Party. Lenin put his trust in the Party as a disciplined striking force, containing people whose occupation was 'revolutionary activity'. In contrast to most Western political parties, which strive for maximum membership, it was fairly narrowly-based and as secret as possible. One fundamental qualification for the Party member was his unhesitating acceptance of Party doctrines, aims, policies and instructions.

Membership of the Party is open to all, but, in practice, aspirants undergo rigorous selection. Recruits are first admitted as 'candidates', that is, probationary members. Only after a year can they be admitted to full membership. The aspirant must have sponsors who are long-standing members of the Party. At one time sponsorship requirements varied according to the social class of the entrant, but, as Russia claims to be a classless society now, these distinctions have been abolished.

To the ambitious Russian, membership of the Party is an honour, and the invitation to join signals his 'arrival' in society. Over the country as a whole fewer than one in twenty of the populace are members. Greater Russians have a somewhat higher proportion than the other Soviet nationalities. Women form less than a quarter of the total membership.

The Party is thus a type of co-optive oligarchy, representing primarily the managerial, administrative and supervisory elements in the Soviet system. About a third of the membership received some form of higher education, this proportion being much higher among the full-time officials and Party secretaries.

Some of the privileges for even lowly members of the Party are quite substantial, for example, renting a country cottage (*dacha*), a holiday on the Black Sea, jumping the queue for buying a new car, a larger apartment. More glittering prizes include foreign travel and access to the 'parallel economy'.

100

The latter term was invented by some Western journalists and commentators who claim that senior members of the Communist Party are allowed to buy Western luxury goods in secret shops. The official is allotted a 'credit' of so many roubles per month depending on his seniority and work performance – a sort of bonus.

Other advantages include privileges for one's offspring. In Western societies these are bought; in the U.S.S.R. they reward steadfast Party service. A hereditary ruling caste has not yet evolved in Soviet Russia, but a citizen's position, power, prestige and pay reflect his level of education, the most important credential both for senior posts and for Party membership. Higher education is in short supply, and influence, naturally through the Party, helps secure a place at university or a special technical school. Wealth is not easily accumulated in Soviet Russia, but the wherewithal for a comfortable way of earning one's living can be transmitted from a Party member to his children.

Although the Communist Party has assumed a complex administrative and economic planning role, it also emphasizes its ideological and indocrination function. Party work is regarded as instruction of citizens whose agreement is essential in the organization and conduct of the state. If the cooperation is withheld repressive measures are instituted, but, as in all political systems, officials are aware that it is easier, more efficient and more productive to govern a people by consent than by coercion. To this end the Russian Communist Party strives to develop a consistent, all-embracing ideology, based on the currently accepted notions of Marxist-Leninist doctrine. This omniscient ideology enables the leadership to silence criticism even if strictures are justified in practice. Dissident opinion suggesting an alternative philosophy is thus potentially very disruptive and has to be vigorously repressed; it threatens the Party oligarchs' unique position as repository of the faith.

Life for the Soviet Citizen

My contacts in Russia have almost all been with professional people, members of the Soviet 'middle classes'. Although their way of life is unrepresentative of the average Russian worker's, it is of interest because many dissidents have evolved from this class.

The Soviet citizen's outlook, values, philosophy for life, and attitude to the outside world all diverge from those of his Western counterpart. The Soviet Revolution is a historical event, its consequences beyond his control. The modification of legal, administrative, political or economic decisions is only a remote possibility. Even decisions about his social and family circumstances are less under his control than they would be in the West. Conformity, at least in action and speech, is necessary for survival, and the Russian learns to interpret the nuances of action or speech of those in authority who guide his life. He wants a quiet life and a predictable future, to avoid officialdom whenever possible, and to keep out of trouble. He is not politically aware (unless he is a Party member), and most of his political pronouncements are official statements rather than individual opinions. He welcomes orderliness and is not mindful of his limited freedom. He accepts internal passports, essential documents to be carried at all times, and the direction of labour which results from the system of residence permits for cities and towns. Freedom and chaos are the same word in Russian. Officialdom is paternalistic towards him, treating him as a simpleton to be indoctrinated, manipulated and protected from deviant elements.

For the intelligentsia, that is, the educated middle classes, Russia is as frustrating to the independent-minded as it was in Tsarist times. The oligarchy ruling Russia is conservative, cautious, at pains to maintain the myth of its infallibility, and deeply distrustful of intellectuals, especially those hankering after foreign ideas. To this end a rigorous censorship is imposed. For example, no foreign newspapers are available except for those published under the imprimatur of Western Communist parties. Jamming of foreign radio broadcasts has been common, though several Russians I met claimed to receive outside news by using short-wave radios. With these exceptions, few Russians were apprised of news such as the true extent of their harvest failures and the purchases of grain from the West.

For the successful and conforming intelligentsia, public recognition is given through awards and honours. Most Soviet intellectuals seem to accept the socialist system and are prepared to observe its rules.

Among scientists the lack of contact with the West has been professionally stultifying. The few that travel freely are selected mainly for ideological rectitude rather than scientific distinction. In the biological sciences, technical advances have been meagre, and claims are made which are difficult to substantiate. The area of research with which I am concerned, the use of drugs in psychiatry, is not highly developed, and I feel no need to scan translations of Russian studies to keep abreast of developments.

Among biological scientists involved in human and social studies the emasculation of research is even more pronounced, because these topics lie within the ambit of political theory. If research findings diverge from predictions from Marxist-Leninist theory, then the research findings must be wrong. Politicians everywhere fervently seize fanciful technological solutions to their economic problems. Usually, however, the scientific establishment, with its predilection for controversy, eradicates spurious claims. In Russia encouragement of politically-motivated opportunists like Lysenko has had tragic consequences, both for other researchers and for Russian scientific progress.

Political Dissension

Action and reaction being equal and opposite, regimes in Russia from Tsarist times onwards have generated much antagonism. And as that opposition has always been suppressed severely, often savagely, unorthodox means of political expression have inevitably evolved.

In Tsarist times terrorism was common, culminating in the assassination of Tsar Alexander II in 1881. On the very day when the bombs were hurled at him, the Tsar had signed an ukase giving Russia a constitution and a form of representative assembly. His successors, Alexander III (1881–94) and Nicholas II (1894–1917), reversed the process of liberalization, and revolutionaries, anarchists and nihilists re-emerged.

With the Revolution, or rather the two Revolutions, March and October 1917, the Bolshevik Communists seized power and paid off old debts. The upper classes were almost eliminated; many fled the country, others were executed. The secret police, the Cheka (actually titled 'Extraordinary Commission for Combating Counter-Revolution and Sabotage'), ruthlessly eradicated opposition from the right.

The Social Democrats (the 'Mensheviks') held office for six months in 1917 but had not tried to regain power after the Bolshevik take-over. They hoped for more freedom, but eventually the Leninist Communists moved against them. Many were allowed to emigrate, but others ended up in the prison camps. The other socialist faction, the Socialist Revolutionary Party, derived its support from the peasants, opposed the Communists, and fomented unrest in the villages. Their leaders were arrested at the same time as the Social Democrats and were arraigned in 1922 in the first of the 'show trials'.

Even before the death of Lenin in 1924, the Bolsheviks were crystallizing into three factions. On the right were 'moderate' Communists such as Bukharin, Rykov and Tomsky, who believed that rapid socialization would cripple Russia and urged some accommodation with capitalism. They defended the policy of slow industrialization with Western investment but were accused of representing the class interests of the private-property and land-owners.

The left opposition was more formidable. Led by the ruthless genius L. D. Trotsky, it urged 'Permanent World Revolution' and advocated intervention in the affairs of other countries by giving support to the local Communist parties. The left demanded rapid industrialization and stern measures against the peasants to siphon off their capital to finance the factories.

In the centre dwelt Josif Stalin. Even before Lenin's death Stalin built up enormous power by his control of the Communist Party's central Secretariat. This influential bureaucratic hierarchy controlled the Soviet Union and represented the interests of the State and Party functionaries.

In the mid-1920s Stalin directed his blows against the left opposition. By allying himself with the right wing, he discredited Trotsky and his supporters. In 1929 Trotsky was exiled and settled in Mexico, where he was murdered by Stalin's agents in 1940. With the left wing demolished, Stalin now initiated its policies of rapid industrialization together with forced collectivization of the peasants: right-wing protests were rapidly silenced. Millions of lives are believed to have been lost in those years; all opposition by the peasants was annihilated. Russian agriculture is still scarred from these wounds.

Both left-wing and right-wing opposition, although enfeebled by imprisonment and banishment to Siberia, still existed, but not for long. The great 'purges' began in 1936, continuing for two years and claiming millions of victims from every walk of life. The remnants of the Social Democrats were wiped out, the left wing disappeared, the right wing vanished. Then Stalin attended to his own comrades. Seventy per cent of his colleagues on the Central Committee of the Communist Party were executed or sent to forced labour camps. An even higher proportion of senior military officers were 'purged', with disastrous consequences when Nazi Germany later encountered Russian armies officered by incompetents and Party hacks. The few survivors of the purges professed unswerving loyalty to Stalin, and the gaps were filled with newcomers owing their advancement entirely to the devious Georgian.

After a slight relaxation immediately after the War, the screw again tightened, and in the late 1940s Stalin introduced yet another reign of terror. His first targets were the Jews with a brutal campaign which crippled Russian-Jewish culture. The newly assimilated territories acquired at the end of the War – Western Ukraine, Western Byelorussia, Estonia, Latvia and Lithuania, Moldavia – underwent the uprooting of any 'class enemies'. Russification of these areas was initiated and all who opposed the process were eliminated as 'bourgeois nationalists'.

The campaigns mounted, and Stalin was probably preparing another major 'purge' to replace one set of henchmen with another group of newcomers who might be trusted for a while. In the Doctors' Plot, several Jewish doctors who attended eminent leaders in the Kremlin were accused of conspiring to poison their patients, including Stalin himself. The trial of these doctors was possibly to be the pretext for generalized terror, arrests, executions and exile to Siberia. On 5 March 1953 Stalin died. His chief hatchetman, Lavrentiy Pavlovich Beria, the head of the Security Service since 1938, was summarily executed. Possibly hundreds of thousands of people were reprieved.

The Post-Stalin era

The death of Stalin heralded some relaxation in the reign of terror, and Khrushchev's denunciation of Stalin at the Twentieth Congress of the Communist Party in 1956 led the opposition elements in Russia to hope that they might influence political events by legal means. The bureaucracy, the main target of the opposition, did partly reform itself but only as a

The Soviet Union and Dissent

grudging concession to mass pressure. Khrushchev tightly controlled the extent and rate of liberalization and reform.

Dissent was permitted provided it was mild, unorganized, unobtrusive and limited in numbers. As soon as any mass movement was discerned the repressive forces were unleashed. If dissenting opinions were stated carefully, usually in the accepted current phraseology of the bureaucracy, there were no harsh reprisals. Thus 'socialist legality' could be observed in 'restoring Leninist norms in the Party and State'. Dissidents could establish contact, voice their heresies, albeit in an indirect allegorical way, and promulgate their ideas among a restricted circle. Contact with Western countries was allowed, especially in cultural and scientific matters.

Relaxation of the pressure produced the greatest explosions in the satellite countries, with uprisings in East Berlin, Poland and Hungary, provoking massive military intervention. The suppression of the revolts in the satellites sparked off a neo-Bolshevik movement in the U.S.S.R., especially among students in the cities. Open protests continued for some time despite the expulsion of hundreds of student activists and the arrest of the 'ring-leaders'. The 'neo-Bolsheviks' called for a return to fundamental Marxist-Leninist principles. They advocated organization of the collective farms into true cooperatives run by their members; workers' control of industry, again providing their own management; the Soviets (local councils) to be democratically elected, truly representative and with real executive power; an end to the repression of political dissidents; freedom of cultural, scientific and political thought and discussion; and though the Communist Party was to remain the sole political party it should become fully democratic, with effective curbs on the power of the bureaucrats. The neo-Bolsheviks believed the Soviet economic system to be more effective than the Western capitalist systems, and they argued that, provided that the political structure could be modified to prevent its manipulation by the exploiting bureaucracy, the Soviet Union would emerge as the strongest country in the world. This opposition was essentially 'within-system', seeking reform *in* but not overthrow *of* the politico-economic structures.

The Last Fifteen Years

In recent years political dissension has ranged from Jews wishing to emigrate and members of national minorities seeking greater self-determination to neo-Leninists protesting against the bureaucracy and to left-wing activists seeking devolution of power to democratically-elected local Soviets.

Underlying these articulate protests is a ground-swell of *economic* discontent among large sections of the population. Soviet Russia keeps its economy on a permanent war footing, and people grow weary of the shortages and austerity, especially when they are constantly reminded of their undoubted economic achievements. Some redeployment of resources from heavy industry to consumer goods is a repeated demand which the authorities eventually have to heed, despite their contempt for the materialist orientation of the Western consumer society. The workers are often hostile towards the privileged bureaucracy and professional classes, who have prior access to scarce consumer goods and to privileges such as foreign travel. The mass discontent is *not* a political movement. It reflects the impatience of the populace with certain aspects of the economy. The system of tied labour on the farms, the lack of money or more usually the lack of anything to spend it on, and the chronic housing shortage in the rapidly growing cities seem to be the main bones of contention.

With Khrushchev's 'thaw' a cultural opposition tentatively developed. There were spontaneous public readings of uncensored work and meetings of like-minded people dissatisfied with the cultural desert of 'socialist realism'. Newsletters were circulated in various cities, and in April 1965 about a thousand young people assembled at a 'literary-political' meeting in order to demand recognition from the official Writers' Union. They asked for the right to set up their own printing press and to have untrammelled public discussions.

As the political controls tightened again, such literary and cultural movements were forced underground. Public discussion was replaced by *samizdat* ('self-publishers') – that is, clandestinely circulating uncensored material, often surreptitiously cyclostyled or laboriously copied by hand. As well as cultural material, a large amount of political matter was also diffused. The *Chronicle of Current Events*, which appeared for several years despite frantic attempts by the K.G.B. to trace its source, was perhaps the best-organized *samizdat*. It provided a wealth of information about political problems, bureaucratic ineptitude and police suppression, none of the allegations ever having been convincingly refuted by the Soviet authorities. Very recently the *Manual on Psychiatry for Dissidents* appeared in *samizdat*; this remarkable document is available in the West.

Khrushchev's relaxation of control in the early 1960s released a flood of information about the atrocities of the Stalinist regime. Many political prisoners were released from the labour camps and others were 'rehabilitated posthumously'. The central authorities, alarmed at this ferment, seized the opportunity presented by the failure of Khrushchev's economic policies to unseat him. The Party reasserted itself, and the clamp-down, seen most overtly in Czechoslovakia, was inevitable.

In 1965 the regime arrested and tried Sinyavsky and Daniel, two *samizdat* writers, leaving the intelligentsia fully aware that dissension was once more impermissible. However, the worst excesses of the Stalinist reign of terror were not reintroduced; there has been greater circumspection in dealing with dissent. In particular, public opinion abroad has to be mollified: first, because the Soviet Union realizes its need for Western technology and in some years American wheat; secondly, because the schism with China has resulted in two Communist ideological systems vying for the hearts and heads of men.

The opposition in Russia has thus not been suppressed, nor

has it subsided spontaneously. A movement of open political public protest has developed, a civil rights movement. It campaigns not for political, economic or cultural change or freedom but for the full implementation of the constitution of 1936, which carefully lists the rights and responsibilities of the Soviet citizen. As in many aspects of life in Russia, there are mechanisms to ensure that the citizen discharges his responsibilities to the State, but the machinery by which he, in turn, exercises his rights is rudimentary, malfunctioning or under the control of the Communist Party. Thus, by crusading for civil rights under the constitution, the political 'opposition' should avoid being accused of anti-Communist activity, crimes against the State, and so on. They are merely petitioning for the implementation of the constitution, drawn up by the authorities and adopted by the controlling organs of the State, including the Communist Party. This tactic of demanding 'within-system' reform does not, however, prevent suppression of the most vociferous campaigners or those least known to the outside world.

Over the past two or three years, even this form of opposition has been rigorously repressed. Nevertheless, various types of dissent have continued, but it must be emphasized that there is no coherent political opposition in the Western sense. Instead, there are many different strands of dissent, some groups with a few aims in common, others with mutually incompatible goals. It is not easy to array these elements along the usual political right–left continuum, since there are components with primarily religious, nationalistic or moral objectives.

With all these disparate elements, mirroring the complex and unusual society from which they stem, organized, unified opposition is not contrivable. No opposition would receive significant *political* support from the mass of the Soviet people despite their *economic* grumbles. Indeed most Russians are openly hostile to dissidents, for in the same way that the established bureaucracy is remote from the Soviet working classes, the intelligentsia comprising the bulk of the dissidents

110

are isolated by virtue of their occupations, attitudes and aims. The average Soviet citizen regards 'the regime as a lesser evil than the painful process of trying to change it' (Amalrik).

The numbers of dissidents cannot be accurately estimated since the term cannot be defined. There are perhaps about a thousand political activists, with a penumbra of sympathizers numbering as many as several thousands at the time of the widespread protests in the mid-1960s. Unlike most radical political movements, students are not heavily involved, perhaps because anyone showing such trends is expelled from his coveted place in the university.

The Treatment of National Minorities

During the seventeenth, eighteenth and nineteenth centuries Russia expanded in all directions but mainly filled the huge void to the East, and in this colonization she incorporated many substantial minorities into her orbit. These minorities, especially Asiatic peoples, were exploited in Tsarist times, the colonization resembling that of the Western European nations except for the absence of any oceanic barrier.

The first and only contraction of Russian territory (apart from selling Alaska to the U.S.A.) followed the Treaty of Brest-Litovsk with the Germans in March 1918, when the western borderlands were surrendered. Only a narrow outlet to the Baltic remained and it was decided to withdraw the capital from Leningrad to the ancient seat of government, Moscow. Finland, intensely nationalistic, achieved full independence.

The Bolshevik government faced two problems, first, to maintain the unity of the sprawling, ramshackle Empire with its numerous minorities and, secondly, to safeguard its western frontiers against the expansionist aims of Germany. At first, separate governments had been set up in the Ukraine and Byelorussia, but eventually Communist control was established and the regions brought into line with Greater Russia.

The Soviet Union claims to be a federal union but not in the sense recognized by the West. The United States of America acknowledges the rights of the individual States in a variety of political, economic and legal spheres, and the States jealously guard their powers. In Russia, any powers possessed by the autonomous republics or regions exist only on sufferance of the central authorities. No indefeasible rights pertain to the federated units, and many organizations and bureaucratic machineries are structured in such a way as to disregard the existence of the federation.

Federalist systems usually endorse the right of any unit to secede, although in practice, as the American Civil War exemplifies, this right is disputed. In the Soviet Union any attempt at secession would be treated as counter-revolution; even ostensibly independent countries such as Hungary and Czechoslovakia are constrained firmly in the Soviet bloc.

Apart from these political considerations, the economic and cultural treatment of the minorities has been less than generous. Greater Russians have been encouraged to move into the peripheral areas, where they are given positions of power and influence. The Kazakhs form a minority in their homeland, Kazakhstan. I was told that less than half the population of Tbilisi, the capital of Georgia, was Georgian. In all regions, Russian is the general second language in education and administration and the Cyrillic script has been introduced for writing most minority languages. A stifling uniformity is being imposed, the objective being complete unity instead of federalism. With the highly centralized nature of the Russian State, and with the bulk of the administrators and technical personnel being Greater Russians, the non-Russian national is forced to assimilate to some degree, especially in the matter of language. There is a pronounced paternalistic attitude of the Greater Russians towards the non-Russian minorities and at times frank discrimination.

It is not surprising, in view of the Soviet authorities' treatment of minorities, that clandestine nationalist movements continue to receive support. The struggle against 'russification' has been most intense, in both cultural and political spheres, in the Ukraine. Several of the political dissidents examined by psychiatric tribunals were Ukrainians arrested for espousing nationalist causes.

Another discontent focuses on the nationalities displaced during the War. Stalin suspected seven nationalities of collaboration or sympathy with the invading Germans. All were deported wholesale under terrible conditions to Siberia and Central Asia. In 1956 it was admitted that the charges against five of the seven groups were unjustified and these peoples were 'rehabilitated' and allowed to return home. The other two national groups, the Crimean Tatars and the Volga Germans, remain in exile.

Religious Dissenters

Marxist-Leninist doctrine being the only true faith, the Soviet authorities have strenuously attempted to eradicate the older-established religions. The first major campaign was initiated in 1918, when Church and State were separated and Church possessions made over to the people. Ten years later, control of all religious associations was tightened and formal religious education of children proscribed. However, some relaxation in the continuous erosion of religious life was allowed in 1941–4, when the authorities acknowledged the role of the Orthodox Church as a rallying point and unifying force for the Russian people. For twenty years there was then an uneasy *modus vivendi* between various religious faiths and the Soviet State, although close surveillance of religious associations persisted.

About 1960 a further wave of repression was instituted against all faiths – Orthodox, Catholic, Baptist, Moslem, Buddhist and Jewish. This time, widespread opposition and dissent were engendered. The exact extent is conjectural, but the signatures on some petitions numbered over 10,000. Over a third of available *samizdat* material is religious in content. Many of the dissidents deemed unfit to plead and sent to prison mental hospitals were arrested for breaking the Soviet penal code relating to religion, such as teaching it to children.

Dissent centres around three issues: religion as an alternative ideology to Communism, the practice of religion as a civil right, and religion as tradition and culture. Each religious minority has somewhat different aims, but all have emphasized the question of ethics and values.

The Orthodox Church

The Russian Orthodox faith has always pervaded Russian life with a deep sense of tradition and messianic mysticism. The Church has stood aside from the mainstream of events in the role of potential saviour. In order to survive it has accommodated itself to the wishes and whims of the authorities, even to the extent of endorsing the obvious falsehood that no obstacles hinder religious observance.

Consequently dissent has appeared in the Orthodox Church, which, since it has 50 million professed believers, is potentially highly disruptive. When the repressive measures of the early 1960s were instituted, opposition slowly intensified, with protests to the civil authorities about the closing of churches and monasteries, the registration of baptisms, interference in church finances, limitation in the numbers of clergy, and so on, all ordinances contrary to the Soviet constitution. Furthermore, some clergy and laymen have protested to the complaisant religious authorities. Significantly, a link has been established between the religious protestants and the Moscow civil rights movement.

The Baptists

This religious group of about half a million were persecuted in Tsarist times and have received similar treatment under the Communists. In 1961 a set of ordinances was issued by the Baptist Governing Council which acquiesced in state interference, control and limitation of evangelical activities. A group of Baptist dissenters issued a counter-document which protested that the Baptist Council was presiding over its own demise and proposed measures safeguarding the theoretical constitutional rights separating Church and State.

As repression of the dissenters proceeded, a secondary wave of protest accompanied the arbitrary arrests, harassments, trials and imprisonments. An organization established to aid the relatives of imprisoned Baptists has succoured prisoners' families, published lists of internees and disseminated information to world organizations.

The Jews

The Jewish problem perplexes the Soviet authorities, whose conduct has been inconsistent and ambivalent. Of all the minorities only the Jews have a homeland outside the U.S.S.R. to which they can emigrate. Many of their protests hinge on their difficulties in trying to exercise their constitutional right to emigrate. At times the Soviet leaders regard the problem as religious, at other times as a national minority issue, and on occasion as an ideological and class question, Zionism representing a Western capitalist subterfuge to subvert a section of the Russian people.

Like other faiths, the Jewish religion was harassed in the 1920s. However, there was no agreement made after the Second World War for it to survive, and the assault in the 1960s was merely an intensification of the persecution of the previous twenty years. Many Jews devoid of any sense of religious identity regained it under the increased molestations. Unable to read Hebrew, they flocked to the few remaining synagogues; isolated from their culture and heritage, they applied to emigrate to Israel. Harassment can be petty, as the following illustrates.

The half-million Jews in Moscow have only two synagogues and no centres of religious instruction. On the High Holy days such as Yom Kippur they congregate at the Great Synagogue, which is in Arkhipova Street in the centre of Moscow near the Kremlin. This building has an imposing classical portico and is beautifully decorated within. Although it is large, the thousands of Jews who gather together out of some sense of common identity cannot be accommodated inside, so they spill out into the road. There was a small grassed area opposite where they could walk, but the authorities fenced this off. The synagogue is in a fairly quiet side road running between two main roads. On Jewish Holy days, the authorities erect barricades across the main road to divert lorries and other traffic down the side road. This prevents the Jews from massing easily in the street, and they are further harassed by police with loud-hailers who keep them on the move. The resulting hubbub can be heard in the synagogue, but a public address system allows the service to be clearly heard by the congregants. Although strictly against Jewish canonical law, this strategem is essential. I witnessed all this on Yom Kippur, 1973, the day the Middle East War started.

The distinguishing feature of Jewish dissent has been its ability to appeal articulately and eloquently to Jewish organizations abroad. International Jewry, long accustomed to supporting Israel, quickly mobilized its influence to assist its coreligionists in the U.S.S.R. American Jews in particular have wrung concessions from the Soviet authorities in direct proportion to the pressure they exerted on behalf of the Russian Jews.

Other Religions

The Moslems, Buddhists and Lithuanian Catholics have all participated in protests and dissent of one sort or another, although not usually as concertedly as the other religious minorities. Links between the various dissenting movements, however, seem to be tenuous. All have been treated harshly by the Soviet authorities, who are as determined as ever to substitute Communist atheism for theistic religions as the Soviet faith.

Overview

Russia remains a country of paradox and tradition. For example, recently some shops have introduced Japanese electronic calculators to replace the abacus, which has been used for calculations for centuries. The cashiers still surreptitiously check the answers on the abacus.

Tremendous economic progress has occurred. Emerging from the Nazi onslaught with her villages and towns ravaged and her industry in ruins, Soviet Russia has rapidly advanced her economy. She is a world power in military and economic terms, and the Kremlin's decisions influence the whole globe.

Life in the Soviet Union has eased materially after the bleak post-war years, and the average citizen enjoys a slowly rising standard of living. He takes pride in Russia's many achievements, especially in space, and is unconcerned about the way of life elsewhere, believing it to be founded on social injustice and political repression. Political expression in the Soviet Union is strictly limited and shows no signs of emancipation.

In most things, we should avoid judging Russia by our own standards. Soviet priorities are different and not necessarily wrong. Policies with emphasis on public rather than private transport, on universal adequate basic accommodation rather than a housing free-for-all, on a steady if limited supply of cheap subsidized food rather than alternating gluts and scarcities, have their non-Communist advocates in the West. That fulfilling these policies seems to be inordinately protracted reflects bureaucratic paralysis, and the absolute priority given to military expenditure.

Nevertheless, certain aspects of human life transcend national boundaries and customs, and these include freedom of expression and conscience and the right to dissent. The Soviet authorities have rebuffed any alternative policies to their own and have harshly repressed anyone daring to oppose them. But still the dissident movements persist.

CHAPTER 8

The Evidence

In 1971 Vladimir Bukovsky's collection of material on the political abuses of psychiatry in the Soviet Union was made available to Western journalists and it has since been published in several languages. Of particular significance are the case-histories of several of the dissidents diagnosed as mentally ill and non-accountable by Soviet psychiatrists. These documents appear genuine: they read like professional case-histories, and no denial of their authenticity has been issued by the Soviet authorities. Furthermore, at the meeting at the Serbsky Institute attended by Western psychiatrists in 1973, the same data concerning the dissidents were presented by the Russian psychiatrists themselves.

For reasons of space I cannot present all the material in detail here. The complete documents have been published in English by the United States Senate Committee on the Judiciary and are available in the United Kingdom. I give the description of the mental state of General Grigorenko in detail, the history of Miss Gorbanevskaya in outline and her published mental state in more detail. The cases of many other dissidents, such as Fainberg, Borisov, Gershuni, Ponomaryov and Yakhimovich, have furnished information but are omitted for considerations of space. Finally, I outline the cases of Plyushch, Bukovsky and Gluzman, three prisoners of conscience.

Wherever possible I have quoted verbatim, so that the informed reader can weigh the evidence himself and compare the case-histories with those of my patients (pp. 45–50). I have commented on the case-histories, and, in particular, state as clearly as I can whether I would have arrived at the same diagnosis.

118

The Case of Pyotr Grigorenko

Biographical note

The following note (as published by the U.S. Senate Committee) was compiled from *samizdat* dissident sources.

Pyotr Grigoryevich Grigorenko was born in 1907 in the village of Borisovka in the Ukraine and was the first in his village to join the Komsomol (Communist Youth League). At the age of 20, he became a member of the communist party of the U.S.S.R.

From 1922 to 1929 he worked in Donetsk as a locksmith whilst attending night school.

In 1929, Grigorenko was admitted to the Polytechnic Institute of Kharkov from which he was transferred, on Party order, as a gifted student, to the Kuibyshev Military Engineering Academy. After his graduation, he served for four years in various units of the Red Army and then was sent to the General Staff Academy to further his military education.

During World War II, Grigorenko distinguished himself as a capable and courageous soldier, and in 1959 was promoted to the rank of major-general. He has been decorated with the Order of Lenin, two Orders of the Red Banner, the Order of the Red Star, the Order of the Second World War, and six medals.

After the end of the war, P. G. Grigorenko worked for 17 years in the Frunze Military Academy, first as chairman of the Department of Scientific Research, then as chairman of the Department of Cybernetics. In 1948, he received the degree of Doctoral Candidate in Military Science and has written more than 60 scholarly works.

In 1961, at a Party conference, General Grigorenko delivered an anti-Stalinist speech. He also wrote an open letter to Moscow voters in which he strongly criticized the 'unreasonable and often harmful activities of Khrushchev and his team.' Khrushchev's reaction was prompt enough. Grigorenko found himself out in the Far East, but he continued to write anti-Government leaflets – with the result that in February 1964, he was arrested, declared mentally disturbed, and sent to a psychiatric asylum where he stayed for 15 months.

While in the insane asylum Grigorenko learned that he had been expelled from the Party, reduced to the ranks, and deprived of his pension. Grigorenko protested, arguing that if he was insane, he could not legally be demoted and deprived of his pension. If, on the other hand, he was sane and guilty of a crime, he should be released and brought to trial. In both cases, he insisted, those responsible for his treatment should be severely punished under the law.

After Khrushchev's downfall, Grigorenko was released, but he was never reinstated. He has written letters demanding rehabilitation to both Brezhnev and Kosygin, but has received no direct answer, except third-party threats of confinement to a psychiatric institution and of suspension of the one-third of his pension which he now receives.

After his release from the hospital, P. G. Grigorenko was unable to find a job and finally was forced to work as a porter. However, he still did not give up his fight against the arbitrariness ruling in his country. He protested against the trials of Sinyavsky and Daniel, of Vladimir Bukovsky, of Yuri Galanskov and Alexander Ginzburg. He led a demonstration before the court building during the trial of the participants of the August 25 protest march against the invasion of Czechoslovakia. He raised his voice in defense of A. Marchenko and I. Belogorodskaya and spoke strongly at the funeral of his friend, writer A. Kosterin, denouncing the totalitarian nature of the regime. He took an active part in the struggle for the rehabilitation of the Crimean Tatars and for the restoration of their republic.

The popularity of the General grew rapidly. He became a real threat to the regime. His activities demonstrated the self-defeating nature of the KGB-inspired kangaroo trials. Each trial gave rise to more protest, more ferment among the liberals and to a further wave of police repressions. The government dared not arrest Grigorenko in Moscow. In all of his actions he strictly observed the laws. The KGB tried to set traps for him and circulated rumors about him and his war record. Finally on May 7, 1969, he was lured to Tashkent where he was supposed to deliver a speech in defence of Tatar leaders who were to be tried there. On his arrival, he discovered that even the date of the trial was not yet fixed. He decided to return to Moscow but was arrested at the airport. Again the KGB tried to proclaim him insane, but the Tashkent Committee of Forensic Psychiatry found him of sound mind. After six months spent in a Tashkent dungeon, where the 62-year-old-man was molested, severely beaten and forcibly fed when he protested his confinement by refusing food, Grigorenko was brought back to

Moscow towards the end of October 1969, for a second psychiatric examination at the ill-famed Serbsky Institute of Forensic Psychiatry. Here he was pronounced mentally ill and sent to the psychiatric hospital-prison in Chernyakhovsk (formerly Insterburg, East Prussia).

In July 1972, Grigorenko was again brought for a psychiatric re-examination. The commission found 'no improvement in his health', and recommended further 'hospitalization'.

Extracts from the records of two psychiatric examinations of General Grigorenko are now presented, as provided by Mr Bukovsky and published by the U.S. Senate Committee. The first was the out-patient forensic examination on 18 August 1969, on the premises of the K.G.B. in Tashkent, Uzbekistan, three months after the arrest in the airport. The second examination was on 19 November 1969 in the Serbsky Institute. The contrasts between the two commissions in the accounts of the defendant's previous activities, his mental state and the conclusions are apparent.

Out-patient Examination, Tashkent, 18 August 1969

Psychological condition: Consciousness clear, correctly orientated. In conversation is perfectly well-adjusted, natural. It is easy to make contact with him. His speech is coherent, purposeful, somewhat pompous. He communicates detailed and consistent information about himself, and in doing so reveals sufficient concentration and memory, a wide and many-sided knowledge of political and social questions, and of questions both of general educational and specialist interest. He declares that all his conscious life he has been interested in the social and political sciences, 'has always been an active political leader and propagandist, had struggled against laxity and lawlessness.' Despite the fact that in the course of his duty he was concerned with technical military disciplines, he considers himself to be better informed on questions relating to the social and political sciences. He describes himself as persevering and active in the attainment of an aim and when 'he comes to some conclusion or other, will not then give it up.'

At the time of the examination he is sufficiently responsive and emotionally alive. To a question about his illegal activities he has an affective reaction, is irritated, becomes red in the face, and in a raised voice tries to prove the rightness of his judgements. Evaluates critically his criminal activity before 1964, when he produced and distributed leaflets and other documents amongst the population. Considers this method of struggle to be incorrect.

In the activities relating to the present charge against him he does not see anything illegal, as he conducted them openly, spoke only for himself, and did not undertake any organizational measures. He shows no confusion, no perceptual delusions. He is painfully and sufficiently aware of the situation which has developed for him. He considers himself a mentally fit person, pointing out that he was upset by the fact of the appointment of a forensic psychiatric commission, as what he fears above all is to be declared mentally ill, to be sent to a psychiatric hospital and to have to live among mental patients. Speaking of this he showed lively emotional reaction, started to weep, but was at once embarrassed, lowered his head, tried to hide his tears, and asked the members of the commission to excuse his 'weakness'.

During the whole of the conversation he retained his courtesy and correctness of behavior.

CONCLUSIONS

Grigorenko at the present time shows no symptoms of mental illness, just as he did not show any in the period of the offences incriminating him (from the second half of 1965 to April 1969), when he understood [the nature of] his activities and was capable of directing them.

In what he did he was of sound mind.

1. Grigorenko's activity had a purposeful character, it concerned concrete events and facts, arose from his personal convictions and in many cases from the same convictions as his fellow-thinkers, and it did not contain sick or hysterical symptoms. All his life Grigorenko has developed correctly from the neuro-psychological point of view, although he has always showed certain original traits of character, such as perseverance in the attainment of a goal, a certain tendency to over-estimate his capabilities, and a desire to affirm his own opinion.

At the same time he has revealed good intellectual capabilities, has through steady effort achieved good general development and stature in the sphere of his work and of socio-community life. He had good relationships in collectives, was a leader and an educator. No appreciable break or damage in the development of his personality has been observed.

It is not excluded that in 1964 under the influence of the psychologically unfavourable situation, and having certain peculiarities of character, Grigorenko suffered a reactive illness assessed in the Serbsky Institute as 'paranoid development.' Subsequently, as is evident from the conclusion of the forensic psychiatrists' commission of experts at the Ministry for the Preservation of Public Order psychiatric hospital in Leningrad, Grigorenko was no longer in a sick condition. Subsequent observation of him in the psychoneurological health center in Moscow revealed no symptoms of psychological illness in him.

2. Grigorenko does not require in-patient investigation, as his personal characteristics and psychological condition are amply described in the document of the case, in data acquired through observation of him in the investigation prison, and also in the data acquired through examination of him as an out-patient.

No doubts concerning Grigorenko's mental health have arisen in the course of the out-patient investigation. In-patient investigation at this time would not increase our understanding of his case, but, on the contrary, taking into consideration his age, his sharply negative attitude to residence in psychiatric hospitals and his heightened sensitivity – it would complicate a diagnosis.

Signed by: Detengof (Professor), Kagan (Chief Psychiatrist of the Turkestan Military District), Slavgorodskaya, Smirnova

In-patient Examination, Moscow, 19 November 1969

Psychological condition: When he entered the Institute and during the first days there, the patient protested at having to undergo the forensic psychiatric examination; was agitated, spoke in a raised voice, declared that sending him to the Institute for diagnosis was an 'arbitrary act', all the more so as the previous, outpatient commission had declared him to be mentally fit. Subsequently the patient became calmer, and made contact with the doctor willingly. During an interview he behaves with a sense of his own dignity, willingly gives information about himself, getting stuck on affectively colored experiences and beginning to talk in a louder tone, his face gradually reddening, his hands beginning to tremble; and he gets into a state of affective excitement.

He considers his struggle absolutely legitimate, and the path he has entered to be the only correct one. When attempts are made to dissuade him he becomes angry and ill-tempered and declares to his doctor that the whole of life consists of struggle, that he had foreseen the possibility of arrest, but that that never stopped him, as he could not renounce his ideas. At the present time he considers himself to be mentally fit.

He formally declares in conversation with the doctor that he does not rank himself among outstanding people and alleges that he does not consider his activity to have historical significance; he says that he acted at the behest of conscience and he hopes that his struggle will not be without effect.

But in his letters, which are among the documents of the case, one finds a clear over-estimation of his own activity and of the significance of his personality and reformist ideas, of the rightness of which he is unshakeably convinced.

In addition he distinctly reveals a tendency to write much and at length, and in his writings it can be observed that side by side with disturbances of the critical faculty he has preserved his former knowledge and ability to present, formally, a consistent account of facts. In his wing of the Institute the patient tries to behave calmly, is polite, sociable, with those around him, and reads literary works.

CONCLUSIONS

Grigorenko is suffering from a mental illness in the form of a pathological (paranoid) development of the personality, with the presence of reformist ideas that have appeared in his personality, and with psychopathic features of the character and the first signs of cerebral arterio-sclerosis.

Confirmation of this can be seen in the psychotic condition present in 1964 which arose during an unfavorable situation which manifested itself in ideas, with strongly affective coloring of reformism, and of persecution. Subsequently, as is evident from the documents of the criminal case and the data of the present clinical examination, the paranoid condition was not completely overcome. Reformist ideas have taken on an obstinate character and determine the conduct of the patient; in addition, the intensity of these ideas is increased in connection with various external circumstances which have no direct relation to him, and is accompanied by an uncritical attitude in his own utterances and acts. The above-mentioned condition of mental illness excludes the possibility of his being responsible for his actions and controlling them: consequently the patient must be considered of unsound mind.

The commission cannot agree with the outpatient forensic psychiatric diagnosis formulated in Tashkent since it has noted the presence in Grigorenko of pathological changes in his psyche recorded in the present report which could not be revealed in the conditions of an out-patient examination because of his outwardly well-adjusted behavior, his formally coherent utterances and his retention of his past knowledge and manners – all of which is characteristic of a pathological development of the personality. Because of his mental condition Grigorenko requires compulsory treatment in a special psychiatric hospital, as the paranoid reformist ideas described above are of obstinate character and determine the conduct of the patient.

Signed by: Corresponding Members of the USSR Academy of Medical Sciences, G. V. Morozov, Professor V. M. Morozov; Professor D. R. Lunts; Senior Scientific Worker Z. G. Turova; Lecturer and Junior Scientific Worker M. M. Maltseva

Comment

Schizophrenia is not mentioned in the formulation, the diagnosis of the Serbsky team being paranoid development of the personality. Both groups of psychiatrists noted essentially the same features: coherent, purposeful speech, great perseverance, over-estimation of his capabilities, a desire to rectify by legal means the anomalies he detects in the Soviet social and political systems.

The Tashkent psychiatrists point out that General Grigorenko's firmly-held convictions were ideas common to his group and that no break in the development of his personality was observed. They concede that, having certain peculiarities of character and being under stress, General Grigorenko might have had a reactive paranoid illness in 1964 but emphasize that if he did he recovered fully.

Professor Detengof and his colleagues see no reason for an

in-patient examination as the case is well-documented and observation detailed, and they humanely recommend against in-patient residence.

The Serbsky team considers that General Grigorenko harbours obstinate reformist ideas, intensified by external events outside his concern (the Crimean Tatars), and accompanied by a lack of self-criticism. They imply that the Tashkent Commission were hoodwinked by Grigorenko's outwardly well-adjusted behaviour but that their own prolonged evaluation has uncovered a mental condition for which compulsory treatment is required 'as the paranoid reformist ideas ... are of obstinate character and determine the conduct of the patient.'

Reformist ideas revolve in a completely circular argument and I cannot accept any diagnosis of mental illness based solely on them. This is the ultimate authoritarian weapon: any impermissible ideas are categorized as delusions.

The case-history bears no evidence of any mental illness, a conclusion bravely stated by the Tashkent Commission. Positions of power and influence are held in most countries by single-minded obstinate individuals who over-estimate their abilities and are opinionated. They are of sound mind and responsible for their actions. So, in my opinion, was and is Pyotr Grigorenko.

One other point: if General Grigorenko's opposition to the regime was deemed to be the non-responsible product of a disordered mind, why was he deprived of two thirds of his legitimate pension?

Postscript: General Grigorenko was released from prison mental hospital in 1974.

The Case of Natalia Gorbanevskaya

Biographical note

The following outline of Miss Gorbanevskaya's personal history is based on the U.S. Senate Committee's publication of *samizdat* sources.

Natalia Gorbanevskaya was born in Moscow in 1936. She finished secondary school in 1952 and entered university as a student of philology. After graduating in 1963 she worked as editor and translator in a Moscow publishing house. In 1965 some of her poems were published in the magazine *Znamya* and the newspaper *Molodoy Komsomolets*.

Her first criticisms of the regime's injustices were poems which the government declared 'decadent' and 'totally unrelated to life'. She became acquainted with Yuri Galanskov and Alexander Ginzburg, who were later put on trial and sentenced for their writings. Miss Gorbanevskaya openly demanded that their trial be public and vigorously protested at the cruel and totally unjustified sentences.

On 25 August, 1968 she joined her friends in a demonstration in Red Square in Moscow, denouncing the invasion of Czechoslovakia by Soviet troops. With the other demonstrators she was assaulted by K.G.B. agents. The protesters were tried and severely sentenced. Miss Gorbanevskaya, however, was declared to be of unsound mind and released into the custody of her mother. She escaped relatively lightly, perhaps because she had two small children.

As the only member of the group not in jail, she began to write a book entitled *Noon: The Case of the Red Square Demonstration of 25 August 1968*, which appeared in *samizdat* and in the West. On 24 December 1969 her apartment was searched. She was arrested and charged with slandering the Soviet Union under Articles 190–91 of the Criminal Code. Seven months later, on 7 July 1970, she was sentenced *in absentia*. The court found her of unsound mind and confined her for an unlimited term to the prison hospital in Kazan.

On 24 February 1972 Miss Gorbanevskaya was finally released. Her friends were elated at her release but at the same time they were appalled by the changes in her. Her personality appeared to have been considerably altered during her 'treatment' in an institution where patients are humiliated, molested, and victimized in an atmosphere of utter sorrow and despair.

On 18 December 1975 Natalia Gorbanevskaya and her two sons left Moscow and arrived in Austria.

The following documents are the conclusion of a commission which rejected the diagnosis of schizophrenia, and extracts from the report of a second commission, five months later, which diagnosed *chronic* schizophrenia.

Conclusion of a Commission presided over by the [Moscow] City Psychiatrist I. K. Yanushevsky, 19 November 1969 [on the condition of N. E. Gorbanevskaya]:

On the basis of a study of the history of the illness, of her medical record over more than ten years and of an examination – there are no grounds for a diagnosis of schizophrenia. Psychopathic personality with symptoms of hysteria and a tendency to decompensation. At the present time, she has no need of treatment in a psychiatric hospital.

Report No. 28/S: The Forensic Psychiatric examination of N. E. Gorbanevskaya, 6 April 1970.
Chairman of the Commission: G. V. Morozov (Corresponding Member of the Academy of Medical Sciences of the USSR); Members of the Commission: Lunts, Pechernikova, Martynenko.

We have the following information from the patient herself and from the legal and medical documents in the case:

Up to the 7th class her school-work was excellent, she was very active in community work. In the 8th class there was a falling-off in her work, she began to be 'lazy'. At home, because of this there was conflict with her mother. Entered the philological faculty of Moscow State University. Worked well. But in her second year she was not allowed to continue as she had missed physical instruction classes; she was afterwards expelled. She herself says in relation to this that from 1955 she experienced a fear of heights and could not perform on the [physical instruction] apparatus.

For a year she did not study, and was in a restless mood. Sometimes she would leave home without any particular motive. Her mother ... observes that her daughter was slovenly, careless about things and about her appearance.

In 1956 Gorbanevskaya for the second time entered Moscow University School of Philology after a competitive examination. In 1957 she was once again expelled for 'missing classes'.

In 1955, for some months before her expulsion, she was in a

depressed state, felt no desire to live, and attempted suicide. She gave as the reason for this attempt at suicide the 'coldness' of the man she loved. Her fear of heights intensified, she could not go upstairs. For two weeks she heard 'voices from the ceiling.' She herself notes that from that time there were changes in her character – she began to be rude to her mother, was irritable, often went away from home to other towns, and there appeared, in her own words, a tendency to 'impulsiveness, to reflex action'.

At the end of 1959 'after overwork' the condition of the patient worsened. She began to have an unpleasant sensation in her fingertips. She could not touch paper or cards and began to be afraid that she would be unable to work. At work she did nothing, would sit for a long time in one position, her hands clenched. Everything irritated her, especially the rustling of paper. She began to suffer from 'a dreadful internal irritability' and insomnia. Then she went to the district psycho-neurologist who made the diagnosis of 'schizophrenia and psychopathy with obsessional features.' From 15 to 30 October 1959 she was in the Kashchenko psychiatric hospital. In the hospital she showed emotional coldness towards her mother and brother, experienced an unpleasant sensation in her finger-tips, could not touch the bedclothes, lay with her hands held upwards. She suddenly asked the doctor for her discharge, saying she was afraid she would become mentally ill through auto-suggestion. After her discharge from the hospital the patient's obsessive thoughts and fears did not leave her, and she visited the outpatient department receiving hypnosis treatment. She was classified as an invalid of Group 3. In 1960 she did not work or study. Her sleep was superficial; at home she could not take part in the household chores.

Subsequently, her condition improved. From 1961 to 1968 she was working very hard on translations by contract. From 1969 onwards she did not have a permanent occupation, but gave private lessons, wrote reviews, and did translations. In February 1968 she had a threatened miscarriage but while in hospital she refused food, was examined by a psychiatrist and transferred to the Kashchenko hospital, where she remained from 15th to 23rd February 1968. During this period no active psychological disorders were observed, but an emotional coldness, languor, and a tendency to moralize were noted. After examination by the chief doctor of the hospital the diagnosis was 'Mild chronic schizophrenia.'

On August 25 she took part in a demonstration in Red Square and was accused under Articles 190–1 of the Criminal Code. After outpatient examination at the Serbsky Institute, the medical team pronounced Gorbanevskaya to be non-responsible with the diagnosis: 'Deep psychopathy; the presence of a mild, chronic schizophrenic process cannot be excluded.' The criminal case against the patient was closed, and she was placed under her mother's care. However, she did not cease her activities and was once again called to account culminating in the present examination.

Psychological condition: The patient is outwardly correctly orientated in relation to the conditions surrounding her, and understands the purpose of her being sent for diagnosis. Converses willingly, calm bearing, a smile on her face. Considers herself a mentally fit person. Is sure that she was sent for diagnosis 'so that there would be no noise', 'because it suited the public prosecutor.' At the same time she does not deny the psychotic episode in the past, considering that she was 'at that time, suffering from a nervous illness.' Her thinking is at times paralogical and inconsistent. Does not renounce her actions but thinks she has done nothing illegal. Unshakeably convinced of the rightness of her actions, she moralizes a great deal, in particular saying that she acted thus 'so as not to be ashamed in the future before her children'. She reveals no anxiety about her own future or the fate of her children, believing that 'her friends will help the children' and 'nothing bad threatens her.' As for writing complaints to the Public Prosecutor, she can't be bothered; to bear the consequences will not be difficult. She talks about everything – her life, her activity, her children – in a monotonous voice. Reveals an unfriendly attitude to her mother, without giving reasons for it. There is an absence of a critical appraisal of her own condition and of the situation which she is now in.

CONCLUSION

Gorbanevskaya is suffering from a chronic mental illness in the form of schizophrenia. Her illness began early in the form of a temporary psychotic episode: fear, auditory hallucinations, motiveless actions. Subsequently it took on a slowly progressive course without evident aggravation but with the gradual growth of personality changes. The present psychiatric examination reveals in Gorbanevskaya the presence of changes in the thinking processes and in the emotional and critical faculties, which are characteristic of schizophrenia. Therefore, as a mentally sick person, and in relation to the actions incriminating her, performed in a state of illness, she must be considered non-accountable. Because of her mental condition and in connection with her persistence of the pathological experiences which determine her conduct, Gorbanevskaya should be sent for compulsory treatment to a psychiatric hospital of special type.

Comment

This is a more complex case, in that Miss Gorbanevskaya had had previous psychiatric admissions. At the age of nineteen she had a fear of heights and went through a phase of depression, a common occurrence in young adults. The symptoms such as 'voices from the ceiling' and unpleasant sensation in the fingertips are not diagnostic, in themselves, of schizophrenia. The irritability and insomnia are more common in depression. The period of stability and hard work from 1961 to 1968 does not fit in with the Serbsky formulation of slowly progressive schizophrenia.

If Miss Gorbanevskaya's case is compared with the two I presented in Chapter 4 (pp. 45–50), it can be seen that there are closer parallels with Miss W.F.J. than with Mr H.P. Both women underwent episodes of unsettled behaviour at university and had philosophical preoccupations. Both expressed their ideas willingly but vaguely.

Miss Gorbanevskaya's mental state at the time of the Serbsky examination is marked by apathy and lack of concern. She 'moralizes a great deal', which presumably means she was concerned with issues of right and wrong. She acknowledged her previous illness but considered herself mentally fit.

I cannot deny that many psychiatrists throughout the world would arrive at the diagnosis of schizophrenia on the evidence presented above. We saw in Chapter 4 how little agreement there is among major centres concerning the diagnosis. Personally I would not have made this diagnosis but would have regarded Miss Gorbanevskaya as suffering from repeated depressive episodes. She appears to have become more depressed during her stay in the special hospital.

Other Cases

I selected the above cases because they both contain the element of disagreement among Soviet psychiatrists, one commission in effect finding the patient sane and not in need of in-patient treatment, the Serbsky commission insisting on compulsory treatment in a special psychiatric hospital.

In Miss Gorbanevskaya's case, the Serbsky commission could at least point to previous psychiatric problems, and it might be questioned whether the Serbsky psychiatrists were guilty of an abuse of psychiatry. In other cases the evidence simply does not survive scrutiny. Yakhimovich struggled 'against a supposedly existing injustice' but at examination 'was polite, gentle, and showed no evidence of delusions and hallucinations': diagnosis – paranoid system in a psychopathic personality. Kuznetsov had a 'critical attitude towards the social system'; at examination 'reformist ideas of a vague, diffuse character': diagnosis – mild chronic schizophrenia. Borisov wrote a letter in defence of Grigorenko; at examination, neurologically normal but 'uncritical attitude to anti-state utterances of the mentally ill in hospital with him': diagnosis – organic cerebral disease (despite neurological and psychiatric normality!).

Reformist delusions are a common finding of the Serbsky psychiatrists. They consist of firmly held wishes to reform the politico-economic system of the U.S.S.R. Of course, if authorities regard the system as perfect, reform is impossible and anyone holding such ideas must be insane. The psychiatrists take the authorities' view and diagnose schizophrenia. A diagnosis based on this feature alone would not be acceptable in the United Kingdom.

The Case of Leonid Plyushch

Leonid Plyushch's case furnishes another example of an apparently sane, well-balanced man being deemed non-respon-

sible and sent to a 'special' psychiatric hospital. So important
was it to suppress information about this mathematician's
case that the hearing was held *in camera*, Mr Plyushch's state
of mind being classified as a state secret.

Detailed accounts by Mr Plyushch and his wife are available
concerning the 'therapeutic' measures he underwent in the
Dnepropetrovsk special mental hospital. In August 1973 treatment was instituted with haloperidol, a major tranquillizer.
Until then Mr Plyushch had retained a high level of intellectual activity and had persevered with his mathematical
studies. After her visit on 22 October 1973 his wife wrote:

> When they brought Leonid Ivanovitch into the visiting room, it
> was impossible to recognize him. His eyes were full of pain and
> misery, he spoke with difficulty and brokenly, frequently leaning
> on the back of the chair in search of support. His effort at self-
> control was evident as from time to time he closed his eyes, trying
> to carry on a conversation and to answer questions. But his inner
> strength was exhausted, finished. Leonid Ivanovich began to gasp,
> to awkwardly unbutton his clothing . . . his face was convulsed and
> he got cramp in his hands and legs . . . It was evident that from
> time to time he lost his hearing . . . Leonid Ivanovich could not
> control himself, and it was he who asked that the meeting be ended
> ten minutes ahead of time. They took him away.

This state is due to the neurological side-effects of the
major tranquillizer. It can be ameliorated by giving medication
(antiparkinsonian drugs), but this was allegedly withheld.
General lassitude and torpor are other side-effects, which can
only be treated by lowering the dose of the tranquillizer.

Leonid Plyushch was abruptly released from hospital and
bundled out of Russia in January 1976 following increasing
pressure from the West, coordinated by several energetic
organizations.

The Case of Vladimir Bukovsky

Vladimir Bukovsky was born in 1942, graduated from Moscow
University's Department of Biophysics and later worked at the
Moscow Centre of Cybernetics.

Mr Bukovsky was first arrested in 1963 after being found in possession of banned literature. He was confined in mental hospitals for twenty months, released in February 1965 but re-arrested later that year for demonstrating in defence of the writers Sinyavsky and Daniel. He was again placed in a mental institution until 1966. In January 1967 he was arrested for the third time, for organizing a protest demonstration against the arrests of Ginzburg, Galanskov and others. He was sentenced to three years' corrective labour.

After his release in early 1970 Mr Bukovsky gleaned information on the abuse of psychiatry in the U.S.S.R. and made it available to Western journalists. Copies of the case-notes of several dissidents were published in the West. Inevitably Mr Bukovsky was arrested for disseminating 'slanderous' allegations against Soviet psychiatry, and in January 1972 he was sentenced to two years' prison, five years in a strict regime labour camp and five years of internal exile for 'anti-Soviet agitation and propaganda'.

After two years in Vladimir Prison he was sent to the labour colony in Perm, where he met Dr Semyon Gluzman. Together they wrote *A Manual on Psychiatry for Dissidents*. For taking part in a hunger strike, Mr Bukovsky was sent back to Vladimir Prison.

Postscript: on 18 December 1976 Mr Bukovsky was released from prison and sent to the West in exchange for the Chilean Communist leader Luis Corvalán. Thus, for the first time, the Soviet authorities tacitly admitted that they had political prisoners.

The Case of Semyon Gluzman

Semyon Gluzman comes from a medical family in the Ukraine. He studied medicine and psychiatry, fulfilling the full training in both subjects.

In 1971 he and two anonymous Kiev psychiatrists published in *samizdat* an unofficial *in absentia* analysis of Pyotr Grigorenko's case, concluding that he was never insane.

In May 1972 Gluzman was charged with 'anti-Soviet agitation and propaganda' on the evidence of *samizdat* documents in his possession. Later that year he was sentenced to seven years in a strict regime labour camp and three years' internal exile. While in Perm labour colony he met Vladimir Bukovsky. Dr Gluzman took part in a hunger strike and lost several privileges for refusing to obey orders.

During the World Psychiatric Association meeting in London in November 1972, protests were made to the Russian visitors regarding Gluzman's case. Both then and subsequently, the Soviet psychiatric and political authorities have denied that Gluzman is a psychiatrist or was sentenced for writing the dissenting diagnostic document on General Grigorenko. However, he was known to some psychiatrists in Moscow, who also informed me that the Soviet establishment psychiatrists were aware of the facts.

Numerous appeals from the West for Dr Gluzman's release have been ignored by the Soviet authorities. Throughout he has retained his courage and his spiritual values, as shown in an uncensored letter to his parents smuggled out of the labour colony: 'I am a Jew, and my Judaism consists in more than memory — the memory of the victims of genocide and of persecutions caused by prejudice become dogma. My Judaism lies in the knowledge of our people as they are today, with their own state, their own history and, happily, their own weapons.'

That 'prejudice become dogma' still oppresses Jews like Dr Gluzman who sustain a conscience become indignation.

CHAPTER 9

Defence, Prosecution and Verdict

In this chapter I deliberately reverse the customary order of prosecution and defence. The allegations against the Soviets are detailed, itemized, and supported by documentary evidence, but the defence of both the Soviet authorities and the psychiatrists are general denials. They do not dispute that political and religious dissidents have broken Soviet laws, been arrested, referred for forensic psychiatric examination, found insane and non-accountable because they were diagnosed as suffering from schizophrenia or paranoid development of the personality, and sent to special prison hospital for treatment. The facts are not challenged. The Russians assert that the diagnoses are made in good faith, the treatments given for genuine illness. Thus their defence is a categorical denial of malpractice; none of the charges are refuted in detail. Consequently I outline the defence first, and then present the particularized allegations, also acting as judge and jury on the detailed points and essaying a verdict. I am acutely aware of my shortcomings in this complex matter, but I owe it to the reader to state the conclusions I have arrived at after many conversations, much reading and a great deal of agonizing consideration and havering doubts.

The Defence

The Soviet authorities have repeatedly denied all the charges that their suppression of political and religious dissidence is harsh and unbecoming to a modern state. They have repudiated accusations that ten-year sentences for circulating *samizdat* material which is constructively critical of the bureaucracy are redolent of twelfth-century Mongol barbarity. Nevertheless, such censure pains the Soviets, particularly the allegations against psychiatry. Officially they have consistently refuted the charges against the Soviet psychiatrists. Both governmental circles and the officers of the All-Union Society of Psychiatrists have refused to acknowledge that either their theory or their practice is imperfect. Indeed, Professor Snezhnevsky stated in 1973 that 'in fifty years of working in the Soviet public health service he knew of no case in which a healthy man was put in a psychiatric hospital.' If that is true, Russia is unique in the world in enjoying the services of infallible psychiatrists.

In conversations with 'establishment' psychiatrists such as Professors Snezhnevsky and G. Morozov (using Soviet translators), I have been impressed by the indignation with which they reject the allegations made against them. They maintain that the political dissidents in special psychiatric hospitals are schizophrenic, according to Russian criteria. When reminded that their criteria differ from those of psychiatrists elsewhere, and are far more inclusive, they answer that many do subscribe to these broad concepts. In a letter to the *Guardian* (29 September 1973) they wrote:

There is a small number of mental cases whose disease, as a result of a mental derangement, paranoia and other psycho-pathological symptoms, can lead them to anti-social actions which fall in the category of those that are prohibited by law, such as disturbance of public order, dissemination of slander, manifestation of aggressive intentions, etc. It is noteworthy that they can do this after preliminary preparations, with a 'cunningly calculated plan of action', as the founder of Russian forensic psychiatry V. P. Serbsky, who was widely known for his progressive views, wrote. To the people around them such mental cases do not create the impression of being obviously 'insane'. Most often these are persons suffering from schizophrenia or a paranoid pathological development of the personality. Such cases are known well both by Soviet and foreign psychiatrists.

The seeming normality of such sick persons when they commit

socially dangerous actions is used by anti-Soviet propaganda for slanderous contentions that these persons are not suffering from a mental disorder.

The Soviet psychiatrists further claim that their view of schizophrenia is supported by their research work, including studies on the family history and immune responses of schizophrenic patients. In fact their research can be adduced as contradictory evidence: clear-cut results were obtained only in patients who were 'core' schizophrenics and who would most probably be diagnosed schizophrenic by Western psychiatrists.

The official refutations by the Soviet psychiatrists run thus: these political and religious dissidents have perpetrated crimes against the Soviet State; however, they are mentally ill on examination and non-responsible for their crimes; they are also not competent to stand trial; as mentally ill individuals they must be treated as in-patients in special hospitals and receive the appropriate treatment.

Prosecution and Verdict

I accept the general truth of the allegations and reject the defence of the Soviet psychiatrists, although I sympathize with their predicament. It is thus simpler to discuss the allegations and my conclusions together.

The evidence substantiating the allegations comes from several sources. The documents sent to the West by Vladimir Bukovsky are notable for their detail and for their psychiatric case-histories. Since 1971, when this material became available, a constant stream of further information has appeared and been publicized. Many organizations and individuals have been involved, including human rights organizations in many countries, Western psychiatrists, jurists, journalists and politicians. Inevitably some political organizations, such as the Russian émigrés, are suspected of bias, and their support of the cause has been exploited by the Soviet authorities, who taunt all concerned people with 'anti-Soviet' motives.

More recently, much material has been provided by patients and ex-patients of the special psychiatric hospitals. They, their relatives and friends have recounted their experiences in memoirs, letters and appeals to the West. Some have left or been expelled from the Soviet Union and have given detailed interviews. Most tellingly, several psychiatrists have left Soviet Russia and have corroborated the testimony of the ex-patients. The consistent detail of these sources strongly supports the authenticity of the bulk of this material. The suggestion that all these people are part of a monumental anti-Soviet conspiracy is risible.

The most prestigious and politically neutral body involved is Amnesty International. In 1975 they published a book entitled *Prisoners of Conscience in the USSR*, which details the allegations. About a quarter of the book concerns compulsory detention in psychiatric hospitals, and I acknowledge my debt to this report for its comprehensive and meticulously documented account of the topic.

The Political Crimes

Almost always, political dissidents and religious adherents are accused of violating Soviet laws. The most notable and well-documented exception was Zhores Medvedev, who was incarcerated in the Kaluga psychiatric hospital without being arrested. Perhaps the real motive was to prevent him from attending an International Symposium on Genetics at the Academy of Sciences Institute of Genetics in Moscow. The crescendo of protest was so deafening that he was released after three weeks.

Political dissidents are generally accused of violating one or more of the following articles of the Soviet Criminal Code.

Article 64: [This defines as an act of treason] flight abroad or refusal to return from abroad to the U.S.S.R.

Article 70: *Anti-Soviet Agitation and Propaganda.* Agitation or propaganda carried on for the purpose of subverting or weakening the Soviet regime or of committing particular, especially dangerous, crimes against the state, or the circulation, for the same purpose, of slanderous fabrications which defame the Soviet state and social system, or the circulation or preparation or keeping, for the same purpose, of literature of such content, shall be punished by deprivation of freedom for a term of six months to seven years, with or without additional exile for a term of two to five years, or by exile for a term of two to five years.

The same actions committed by a person previously convicted of especially dangerous crimes against the state or committed in wartime shall be punished by deprivation of freedom for a term of three to ten years, with or without additional exile for a term of two to five years.

Article 72: *Organizational Activity Directed to Commission of Especially Dangerous Crimes against the State and also Participation in Anti-Soviet Organizations.* Organizational activity directed to the preparation or commission of especially dangerous crimes against the state, or to the creation of an organization which has as its purpose the commission of such crimes, or participation in an anti-Soviet organization, shall be punished in accordance with Articles 64–71 of the present code.

Articles 190–91: *Circulation of Fabrications known to be False which Defame Soviet State and Social System.* The systematic circulation in an oral form of fabrications known to be false which defame the Soviet State and social system and, likewise, the preparation or circulation in written, printed or any other form of works of such content shall be punished by deprivation of freedom for a term not exceeding three years, or by correctional tasks for a term not exceeding one year, or by a fine not exceeding 100 roubles.

[Religious prisoners are usually prosecuted under Articles 142 or 227.]

Article 142: *Violation of Laws on Separation of Church and State and of Church and School.* The violation of laws on the separation of church and state and of school and church shall be punished by correctional tasks for a term not exceeding one year or by a fine not exceeding 50 roubles.

The same acts committed by a person previously convicted of violation of laws on the separation of church and state and of school and church, as well as organizational activity directed to the commission of such acts, shall be punished by deprivation of freedom for a term not exceeding three years.

Article 227: *Infringement of Person and Rights of Citizens under Appearance of Performing Religious Ceremonies.* The organizing or directing of a group, the activity of which, carried on under the appearance of preaching religious beliefs and performing religious ceremonies, is connected with the causing of harm to citizens' health or with any other infringement of the person or rights of citizens, or with the inducing of citizens to refuse social activity or performance of civic duties, or with the drawing of minors into such groups, shall be punished by deprivation of freedom for a term not exceeding five years or by exile for a similar term with or without confiscation of property.

The active participation in the activity of a group specified in paragraph one of the present article, or the systematic propaganda directed at the commission of acts specified therein, shall be punished by deprivation of freedom for a term not exceeding three years, or by exile for the same term, or by correctional tasks for a term not exceeding one year.

Note. If the acts of persons stated in paragraph 2 of the present article, and the persons themselves, do not represent a great social danger, measures of social pressure may be applied to them.

Both political and religious dissidents are familiar with the risks. They witness the fate of their colleagues and may receive preliminary cautions from the K.G.B. or more informal admonitions from their superiors at work. The swingeing five- and ten-year sentences may appear of Draconian severity, but dissenters are inured to them as the 'going rate'. Although the political dissidents often protest the illegality of the charges, they bear no illusions about the reality of the outcome. Nor can they usually emigrate if conditions in the U.S.S.R. become too intolerable.

The Soviet authorities do not acknowledge political dissent, so that individuals accused of violating the above articles are considered criminals, not political prisoners. Similarly, people charged with breaking the laws about religion are not distinguished from criminal offenders.

The acts leading to the charges against the political dissenters usually have indeed taken place. Banners censuring the Soviet invasion of Czechoslovakia were briefly unfurled in Moscow; *samizdat* documents calling for the implementation of the Soviet constitution were found in the homes of some dissidents; some applicants to emigrate to Israel possess Zionist literature; religious people like the dissenting Baptists congregate to sing hymns and keep tape-recordings of sermons.

The usual practice is to repress severely any signs of dissent. To this end, the existing laws are interpreted harshly, or on occasion deliberately distorted. Apparently innocuous *samizdat* is construed as serious anti-Soviet slanders, the possession of non-official documents being the real crime to the Soviet authorities.

Once a dissident has been noticed by the K.G.B., he risks being accused of anti-Soviet activities. If he has been previously convicted of such activity, K.G.B. surveillance will be protracted.

Why are the Soviet authorities so intolerant of criticism, ideological deviation and religious loyalties?

In brief, political freedom has never taken root in Russia, the autocracy of the Tsars being replaced by the oligarchy of the Bolsheviks, the absolute despotism of Stalin and the dictatorship of the Communist Party. Religious dissension has also never been tolerated, the pogroms against the Jews and the persecution of Baptists being officially encouraged into the present century. Marxist political and economic theory claims to explain all politico-economic institutions, to predict their development or decline, and to offer an alternative and superior system. The Marxist system is reckoned by its adherents to be perfect in conception, and any shortcomings must therefore be ascribed to malign external influences, such as Western capitalism, or to internal saboteurs. Anyone not accepting *in toto* the current orthodoxy in theory and practice falls into the latter category. The Soviet Marxist-Leninist system must be spotlighted as functioning more efficiently and more equitably than the rival systems of capitalism or mixed economies, so that the Soviet system inevitably triumphs, the proletariat in other countries clamouring for the Revolution. Anyone alluding to obvious deficiencies in Russian economic performance, harvest failures, lack of political expression, denial of basic human and civil rights, is a traitor to Marxism. Since Soviet Russia, economically and politically, is on a permanent war footing, political dissenters are dealt with appropriately – as if they had gravely sabotaged the war effort.

Religious prisoners of conscience often accept the political and economic dogmas but maintain their loyalty to an ideal. People observing the rituals of religious practice are viewed as threats to the purity of Marxist-Leninist dogma. Because parents can influence their children before they are exposed to political doctrines, they must be dissuaded from religious instruction. Because religious meetings are imbued with a spiritual quality transcending political assemblies, such groups must be dispersed. Because religious literature excites quintessential sentiments and longings for the immaterial, it must be excised and destroyed.

And yet, of those in psychiatric prisons, the religious prisoners of conscience are most resistant to the pressures. Toughened by confinement, annealed in spirit, these modern martyrs emerge to resume their faith.

Arrest and Interrogation

Arrest and interrogation are controlled by the investigating officials, who in the case of alleged political crimes are K.G.B. personnel. Although (as outlined on pp. 90–91) the Procurator's Office can oversee and sanction arrests, in practice the K.G.B. acts more or less autonomously. Procedural guidelines are usually followed, but local excesses of zeal often occur, with contemptuous disregard for the basic human rights of political and religious detainees. For example, Jonah Kolchinsky, a nineteen-year-old Jew from Kharkov who had applied to emigrate to Israel, was beaten up by the police in his home and on the way to the police station, where during twenty-four hours without food he was subjected to anti-semitic gibes.

The arrest may be made immediately after the alleged offence, such as taking part in a demonstration, or it may be delayed pending further investigations. Searches of apartments or places of work are commonplace and are often unauthorized by higher legal (rather than K.G.B.) authority.

Pre-trial detention should not exceed nine months, the Procurator's Office being responsible for ensuring that the detainee is either brought to trial or released if the preliminary investigation oversteps this limit. Nevertheless, a year or more has elapsed before the arraignment of some political prisoners. Leonid Plyushch was arrested in January 1972 and brought to trial in January 1973, the extension being formally approved by the Supreme Soviet. In instances where the accused is referred for a forensic psychiatric examination, the interval between arrest and sentence is commonly prolonged.

During pre-trial detention, visits by family and friends are entirely governed by the examining officials. Communication with a legal representative is also under their regulation. Bail is almost unknown.

Referral for a Psychiatric Examination

The decision to request a forensic psychiatric examination of the accused depends on the officials investigating the case. In fact they are obliged to make the request if they suspect the accused to be mentally ill.

In practice such an examination is ordered on a variety of pretexts. If the accused has any psychiatric history or past treatment, he is likely to be referred even if the previous episode was trivial or transitory, such as a childhood fear of heights or a brief episode of insomnia and anxiety following a stressful incident at university. Secondly, the investigating officials may request a psychiatric examination if the accused is emotionally upset on arrest, tearfully insisting his innocence and claiming wrongful arrest. Conversely, fatalistic acceptance of arrest and indifference to the inexorable outcome have also been interpreted as evidence of an insidious and otherwise covert mental illness. Finally, the more extreme the protest, the more likely are the protesters to be subjected to a psychiatric assessment. Public demonstrations particularly upset the K.G.B., which uses the argument: 'If he opposes the regime so provocatively, he must be mad.'

Why should the Soviet authorities be so zealous in referring dissidents for a psychiatric opinion? After all, prisoners accused of breaking certain articles of Soviet law can be effectively sentenced in the criminal courts in the usual way. According to Amnesty International, no person in the Soviet Union accused of a political offence has ever been acquitted. There is thus no danger that the charges will be dismissed. Furthermore, the length of time which dissidents after trial spend in special psychiatric hospitals is about equal to that which their 'sane' colleagues spend in prison, so the duration of the dissident's removal from active political or religious life does not rest on the mode of 'disposal'.

There are probably several reasons, varying in their relative importance from case to case. First, a totalitarian state finds it expedient for the strictures of its critics to be not merely quashed as heretical but also dismissed as the incoherent ravings of lunatics. The more extreme the protest or the more pertinent the criticisms, the stronger the temptation to have the dissenters deemed mentally incompetent. As a bonus the views of the associates of dissidents declared insane will also be denigrated in the eyes of the passive majority.

Secondly, the legal proceedings against the accused are greatly simplified if he is found incompetent to stand trial. He retains no real rights and can merely hope for an honest hearing in the court. However, the court is not obliged to allow the accused to appear or to defend himself. Consequently the authorities can prevent the accused from making a dramatic court statement which would be relayed to other dissidents via the *samizdat* system and eventually percolate through to the Western press. When the accused is deemed incompetent he can be removed from the dissident circles with the minimum of fuss.

Thirdly, the authorities often seem spiteful in taking full advantage of the fact that an intelligent individual is distressed when he is officially diagnosed as mentally ill. The *Manual on Psychiatry for Dissidents* by Bukovsky and Gluzman stresses this:

Dissidents, as a rule, have enough legal grounding so as not to make mistakes during their investigation and trial, but when confronted by a qualified psychiatrist with a directive from above to have them declared non-accountable, they have found themselves absolutely powerless. All this has, inevitably, engendered renewed fear and dismay in dissident circles and is the reason for cases of unexpected 'repentance' and renunciation which have occurred in recent months. Forensic psychiatry has thus renewed the fear of persecution, which a knowledge of the law and skill in applying it had previously dispelled. A mood of resignation to one's fate, a sense of one's powerlessness to resist this method of persecution, has become widespread.

A fourth factor is that the length of time for which a dissident declared insane can be committed to a mental hospital is indefinite. He has none of the meagre rights of a prisoner but is under the total control of the authorities administering the mental hospital. He can be 'treated' against his will and can be locked up with severely mentally ill and dangerous patients.

The Forensic Psychiatry Commission

The Soviet authorities assert that the forensic psychiatry commission reaches an independent, objective and expert opinion on the case before them, and that the interests of the accused are safeguarded because the doctors are not only bound by a professional oath but are enjoined by law to act correctly.

The forensic psychiatric examinations are carried out under the auspices of the Ministry of Health, but several considerations throw doubt on their disinterestedness. The investigation officials, the Procuracy and the K.G.B., decide which experts will conduct the examination. They can appoint the members directly but usually they nominate an appropriate institution which has a panel routinely available. The examining officials also prepare the case-material for the commission and can ask it specific questions. The accused and his relatives have no psychiatric representative on the commission.

The Serbsky Institute, under its director Georgy Morozov, is in effect the final arbiter in many political cases. Typically it is involved if the accused lives in Moscow or committed his offence there, or if a local forensic psychiatric commission has the temerity to find the accused sane. This happens occasionally, as in the case of General Grigorenko (Chapter 8), but immense pressures are brought on the psychiatrists in provincial mental hospitals to find non-accountable political or religious dissidents referred by the examining authorities. Not only are the psychiatrists state employees – as in many other countries – but the authorities, both locally and nationally, reckon that their interests over-ride moral and professional scruples. The coercion on the psychiatrists in these local commissions betrays the desire of the authorities to have political dissidents deemed unfit to stand trial.

The sanctions that can be used against Soviet psychiatrists are many and widespread, but also diffuse and difficult to document. A major one is postponement of promotion. As senior posts in the Soviet Union involve more privileges as well as increased salary, deferment can be very disadvantageous. Even more deleterious is demotion, which has been used, for example, against Jewish psychiatrists who applied to emigrate to Israel: following 'reorganization' of their hospitals or institutes they found themselves relegated to junior posts in local dispensaries. In major instances of defiance, such as Dr Gluzman's publication of an alternative diagnosis on General

Grigorenko, a charge of anti-Soviet activities, with inevitable imprisonment and exile, is the ultimate sanction. There is only one Gluzman among the Russian psychiatrists, but his courage is widely recognized among his colleagues.

The most ubiquitous pressure makes use of people's reluctance to be identified as 'uncooperative' in political matters. So many areas of Soviet life are governed by arbitrary executive decisions against which there is no appeal, legal or administrative, that a question-mark against a psychiatrist heeding his conscience heralds subtle but nonetheless irksome consequences. The pusillanimous psychiatrist accommodates the wishes of the K.G.B., especially if his immediate superior has already succumbed or, as a loyal Communist Party member, is eager to accede to his colleagues' wishes.

Dr Marina Voikhanskaya, who worked as a psychiatrist in the U.S.S.R. before coming to the West, befriended a dissident artist named Ivanov in her hospital and took him books and cigarettes. She was shadowed on her way to work by a car with a uniformed chauffeur and on one occasion was deliberately almost knocked over. The hospital director shouted at her for two hours, threatened her with dismissal and demanded that she cease her visits to Ivanov. She was ostracized by her colleagues, 'isolated in a vacuum'. Several psychiatrists, previously close friends, avoided her. Dr Voikhanskaya concludes: 'Doubtless there are many worthy people among the psychiatrists in my hospital, but I never managed to discover who they were.'

That forensic psychiatric commissions do on occasion declare that an accused is sane and fit to stand trial testifies to the sincerity, integrity and bravery of these psychiatrists. Few people in the West realize the significance of these cases: some psychiatrists in the U.S.S.R. are manifestly functioning independently, as in the cases of Grigorenko and Kuznetsov, despite the obvious wish of the K.G.B. that the dissidents be found insane.

I deprecate the Soviet authorities' remorseless pursuit of the arrested political dissidents as shown by the referrals to the

Serbsky Institute. At the Institute, politics and psychiatry seem to be inextricably confounded. The so-called 'Special Section' includes representatives of the K.G.B. This is superficially no more remarkable than some British doctors belonging to the Territorial Army, a part-time defence force. However, the K.G.B. sways the activities of the institutions in which it has a presence. Although the Serbsky Institute is nominally under the aegis of the Ministry of Public Health, its Special Section under Professor Lunts is K.G.B.-orientated.

The head of the Serbsky Institute, Professor Georgy Morozov, is large, bluff and hearty; with his rubicund face he would pass as a dairyman. He speaks broken English and made little contact with Westerners on the two occasions I met him. When disputing the allegations against Soviet psychiatrists, he seemed less indignant than his non-forensic colleagues. When he discussed concepts of schizophrenia, his capacity for acknowledging the fallibility of psychiatrists seemed limited. However, it is impossible to secure a just impression of someone whose conversation is being filtered through an interpreter.

General Grigorenko observed Professor Lunts, the head of the Special Section, coming to work in the uniform of a K.G.B. colonel. I have not encountered this *éminence grise* of the Serbsky but I have been assured that he is a K.G.B. officer as well as a psychiatrist, and that other members of his section, doctors and nurses, hold K.G.B. rank. The odious reputation of Lunts and his minions in dissident circles is well-documented, as is his steadfast public support by Professor Morozov. Both are frequent signatories to forensic commission reports.

The Diagnoses

Recall the two aspects of the deliberations of the psychiatric commissions: the demonstration of mental illness in the accused, and establishing whether he is therefore incapable of standing trial.

Forensic psychiatric commissions, especially that of the

Serbsky, usually arrive at one of two diagnoses: creeping schizophrenia or paranoid development of the personality. Creeping schizophrenia corresponds roughly to simple schizophrenia in Western European diagnostic classifications, but it is a dubious entity in the absence of firm evidence such as a steadily downward course plus psychotic features such as *bizarre* delusions and hallucinations. Some Soviet psychiatrists assert that the most subtle forms of creeping schizophrenia present diagnostic problems soluble only by major experts such as the Serbsky personnel. The symptoms of these insidious forms of schizophrenia include unsociability, loss of interest, episodes of pessimism and sluggishness, concentration on ideas, obstinacy and rigidity of convictions and ideas, and suspiciousness. These are regarded as signs of insidious schizophrenia despite the absence of major symptoms such as thought interference and despite the patient's coping successfully with work, family relationships and leisure activities.

There is no scientific basis for these claims. Indeed it is an elementary logical error to conclude that, because a seriously ill schizophrenic patient may be 'sluggish', depressed, suspicious and unsociable, an otherwise healthy person with minimal tendencies of this sort must be suffering from a mild form of the illness. One might as well argue that because severe cough is a symptom of pulmonary tuberculosis, then anyone clearing their throat repeatedly is suffering from mild T.B. Schizophrenia is not a clearly defined entity, but there are sufficient typical features to aid diagnosis. The *form* of the 'illness' in the dissidents lends no support to the diagnosis of 'schizophrenia' by the Soviet psychiatrists in the forensic commissions.

The second diagnosis, paranoid development of the personality, is even more vague and unspecific. As the condition is predicated as a *personality* development, there cannot be an 'illness' in the medical sense. The normal person develops unsociability, rigid, sluggish thought-processes, fixations on certain ideas and mistrustfulness. As in 'sluggish schizophrenia', abrupt changes in the person's psychological functioning are absent. The condition is presumed because of certain exaggerated personality traits. There is neither *form* to this condition, nor major symptoms, nor well-defined onset, time-course or prognosis.

If the form of neither 'sluggish schizophrenia' nor 'paranoid personality development' can be defined, what about the *content* of the 'illness'? Is this a sufficiently reliable basis for a firm and justifiable diagnosis? As we saw in earlier chapters, certain symptoms are especially portentous. For example, if a patient claims that men from Mars are etching important messages on the inside of his skull, and the messages are unintelligible and bizarre, the diagnosis of schizophrenia is likely and would be upheld by almost all psychiatrists. However, none of the case-histories of the dissidents contain such features and I know of no claim by any Soviet psychiatrist that such symptoms have been elicited in any political or religious dissident. Instead, the usual claim is that the patient has 'reformist' delusions or 'litigation mania'. We must therefore examine such assertions in the light of our discussion of delusions in Chapter 3 (pp. 25–8).

The identification of a delusion is a matter of the opinion of the psychiatrist, who bases his conclusion on the incorrigible nature of the idea and its inappropriateness to the individual's background and previous beliefs. To rest the diagnosis of a delusion solely on the content of the firmly-held belief exposes psychiatrists to the charge that they are acting as society's suppressors of heterodox ideas. When these beliefs are political or religious, the danger increases. Sometimes, of course, the belief is manifestly absurd and held to be so by close political colleagues or co-religionists of the individual. The really original thinker has always invited ridicule by his associates, and if he purveys his ideas with single-minded determination he may be labelled mad. However, such people are rare and psychiatrists can perhaps be forgiven for being as stupid as the rest of mankind in deriding them.

In theory, small groups of individuals with common beliefs pose problems. However, as usually no law is broken, most societies tolerate such collective eccentricity and the psychiatrist is not required to examine members of these sects.

Where the crime consists of political utterances or acts or of religious activities such as organized hymn-singing, the state of mind of the accused then concerns the psychiatrist. In the Soviet Union, forensic psychiatrists must examine the alleged crime and the patient's state of mind in an attempt to relate the two sufficiently to answer the question: 'Was the accused's speech or behaviour the consequence of mental illness and is medical treatment indicated to prevent such behaviour in the future?' Inevitably, the Soviet psychiatrist must assess the 'crime' for its political or religious content in order to establish whether the beliefs arose from a disease process ('schizophrenia', for example) in the patient's brain. The Soviet psychiatrist cannot side-step the content of the dissenting belief but is required by the terms of reference of the examining authorities to juxtapose these beliefs and the previous upbringing and conduct of the patient.

Some Soviet psychiatrists have few illusions as to their role in these examinations. They state ingenuously that dissident political beliefs are regarded by the authorities as socially dangerous and that people with such beliefs will find themselves in a special psychiatric ward. For example, one psychiatrist allegedly said to Mr Borisov 'Listen, Borisov, you're a normal fellow and I am sure you don't want to be sent to a madhouse. Why don't you change your views?'

Other Soviet psychiatrists do not accept politically deviant views or a firm religious persuasion as signs of mental illness, and, as we have seen, such psychiatrists have reported dissenters referred to them to be perfectly sane. At the other extreme are the Serbsky psychiatrists, who detect 'reformist delusions' in dissidents. This argument is untenable, as the only evidence that these ideas are delusions is that they are reformist in content. When challenged, the Serbsky psychiatrists shelter behind the cult of the expert, as in their letter to the *Guardian* on p. 137.

They claim that a subtle form of schizophrenia or paranoid

personality is manifested by anti-social acts alone. But other widely-accepted signs of mental illness should be present: *it is not possible for a diagnosis of mental illness to be arrived at solely on the basis of deviant political or religious beliefs.* The Serbsky myrmidons are unscientific in their lack of firm criteria for mental illness, illogical in their assumption of mental illness on the sole basis of anti-social acts, arrogant in their dismissal of the 'seeming normality' of the dissidents, and careless of the reputation of psychiatry.

There is one final argument against the validity of 'reformist ideas' as evidence of mental illness. Many political and religious dissidents in the civil rights movement limit their demands to implementation of the Soviet constitution. This was drawn up by the Soviet authorities under Stalin's guidance and ratified by the Supreme Soviet. If urging adherence to its bright ideals is evidence of reformist tendencies and thus of mental illness, the Soviet authorities who have sustained the fiction of this constitution for forty years are party to this grand delusion.

However, the issue is not just the diagnosis of mental illness but whether the accused is capable of standing trial. Many mentally ill patients are perfectly capable of appearing in court and conducting their defence. However, once the diagnosis of mental illness is made in the Soviet Union, the inevitable and paternalistic consequence is the assumption that the prisoner must be protected by not being allowed to stand trial. I do not know of any dissidents deemed to be suffering from mental illness who were deemed capable of pleading.

The Trial

The decision to refer an accused individual for a forensic psychiatric examination greatly simplifies legal procedures and deprives the accused of almost all his rights. For example, he need not be informed that his state of mind is to be evaluated nor is he notified of the commission's findings. He has no right to challenge the medical findings.

The court proceedings need not be public if the accused is deemed unfit to plead. While ostensibly a humane measure to spare an insane person public obloquy and derision, this regulation can conveniently prevent reporting of court proceedings. The relatives and friends of the accused can be excluded from the *in camera* proceedings. Even the accused has no right of appearance before the court. It is entirely at the court's discretion who stands before it and the accused cannot even submit a written statement without the court's permission. Thus dissidents have been deemed insane and sentenced without their knowledge.

As the accused cannot defend himself, the law states that a defence counsel must attend the court as a safeguard. Even so, defence counsel is not required to meet his client but may work solely from the written documents. Defence counsel in the Soviet Union in political cases are supine individuals who limit their operations to pleading mitigating circumstances for their clients. On rare occasions defence counsel have been more active but have suffered: thus the advocate Zolotukhin was expelled from the Party and the Collegium of Advocates for 'adopting a non-party, non-Soviet line' in the defence of Alexander Ginzburg. I am not aware of any Soviet lawyer opposing the psychiatric opinion given to the court. Usually defence counsel contents himself with unctuously praising the court for its humane treatment of the accused.

As the psychiatric opinion is advice to the court and there is no adversary system of expert evidence, the conclusion is usually accepted unchallenged and unmodified. The opinion is usually accompanied by a recommendation that the accused be confined in a psychiatric hospital until cured of his 'dangerous anti-social ideas'. The courts almost invariably order the compulsory detention of political dissidents in special psychiatric hospitals which are reserved for those representing special dangers to society. Confinement is for an indefinite period until recovery.

Special Psychiatric Hospitals

There are at least nine special psychiatric hospitals in the U.S.S.R., situated in Leningrad, Sychnovka near Smolensk, Minsk in Byelorussia, Dnepropetrovsk in the Ukraine, Kazan in the Tatar republic, Chernaykhovsk near Kalingrad, Blagoveshchensk in the Soviet Far East, Kzyl-Orda in Kazakhstan, and Oryol in Oryol region. The Kazan institution takes all the female patients. The Sychyovka hospital is the most notorious among former inmates.

Prisoners in the U.S.S.R. have certain rights itemized in the legal code and can protest, sometimes effectively, when these rights are ignored. Patients in the special psychiatric hospitals have no such rights, and the hospitals are governed by ministerial regulations. Patients in these hospitals are regarded as incapable of managing their own affairs, and there is no procedure whereby they can seek redress for any medical or legal excesses committed against them. They are literally at the mercy of the hospital staff. Furthermore, communication with the outside world is strictly controlled. Letters to relatives are permitted only at the doctors' discretion and must not mention medical treatment or hospital conditions. Patients may not contact lawyers or the Procuracy, although the latter are responsible for supervising these institutions.

In the U.K., the special hospitals like Broadmoor are administered by the Department of Health. In Russia these special psychiatric hospitals are managed by the internal security forces (M.V.D.). The inevitable inference is that in operating these establishments medical factors are subordinated to security considerations. This is deleterious to those inmates who have criticized such aspects of Soviet political life as the immense power of these internal security forces.

The hospitals are usually former prisons surrounded by barbed wire. The medical staff hold ranks in the M.V.D., and the warders are members of the security forces. The orderlies, however, are recruited from convicted prisoners in the corrective labour institutions. These untrained convicts are notorious for ill-treating the patients. The Amnesty International Report documents the systematic and sadistic ill-treatment which the orderlies and warders dispense to the patients with the 'silent approval of the nurses and obvious connivance of the doctors'. Jewish inmates are particularly persecuted.

The medical staff, even if they were greatly concerned, would find it difficult to protect the patients. There are two systems of control in these hospitals: one is the medical chain (physician-superintendent – head of the section – psychiatrist directly in charge – nursing staff); the other is the security personnel down to the warders. The medical staff exercise no authority over the warders, which exemplifies the minor role of treatment compared with security and unauthorized punishment. If treatment was the prime aim, other considerations would be geared to it.

It is difficult to estimate the number of political and religious dissidents held in special psychiatric wards. About 120 are known to Amnesty International, but Mr Plyushch has stated that there were about sixty in his hospital alone. Multiplied up, this would suggest a total of several hundreds.

'Treatment'

The doctors too are accused of resorting to their own form of punishment under the guise of 'treatment'. The patients cannot question their treatments nor can their relatives demand information, even about the psychiatrists' identity. The patients are almost totally isolated and are forced to undergo treatments which they have had no opportunity to discuss with their own doctors or relatives. This suggests an arrogant disregard for basic human rights in these Soviet special psychiatric hospitals.

The most reprehensible practice is the systematic use of major tranquillizers in unnecessarily large doses. No one disputes that these drugs can induce distressing and even dangerous side-effects, especially in patients with minimal disturbance and in normal individuals. The latter can be upset by small doses, as I can testify from personal experience and from experimental observations, whereas a disturbed patient may be hardly affected by ten times the dosage.

The earliest signs of excessive dosage are a profound lassitude and torpor. Any will to read, to concentrate, to pursue intellectual activities is dissolved. The individual sits inert, inactive, vegetable-like; sleepiness may be profound and the patient drowses for days on end, as did Leonid Plyushch (see p. 133).

The next effects are the various 'extra-pyramidal' actions of the drugs (see also Chapter 5, p. 63). The most dramatic, which may ensue after a single dose or during the first few days of treatment, consists of acute muscular spasms. The head may be pulled back or twisted to one side or the jaws locked shut in painful spasms. The patient may be unable to stand or walk because of spasms in the legs or back. These drug effects can be quite easily treated, and the dosage should be reduced.

Another form of muscular impairment is pseudo-parkinsonism. This mimics the disease occurring spontaneously in old age, characterized by immobility and lack of voluntary movement together with a distressing trembling of the fingers. The sufferer is quite clear in his mind and yet appears to be a slavering idiot. The major tranquillizers in large doses induce this clinical picture quite readily, but again lowering the dose or administering an antidote is a potent preventative.

The third condition akathisia, is a marked restlessness of mind and body. Inexperienced psychiatrists sometimes mistake it for schizophrenic agitation and increase the dose of tranquillizer instead of lowering it. The political dissident Mr Gershuni wrote a clear account of akathisia: 'This medicine [chlorpromazine and haloperidol] makes me feel more awful than anything I have experienced before; you no sooner lie down than you want to get up, you no sooner take a step than you're longing to sit down, and if you sit down, you want to walk again – and there's nowhere to walk.'

However, the most appalling extra-pyramidal effect of the

major tranquillizers is 'tardive dyskinesia'. This condition may supervene after a few years' treatment, especially in the elderly, though it is not unknown after only a few months in young patients. It is characterized by repeated, persistent mouthing movements, pursing of the lips and grimacing. Unlike the other three types of movement disorders outlined above, the dyskinesia may persist when the drugs are stopped. Thus political or religious dissidents given major tranquillizers as 'treatment' for their 'schizophrenia' run the real danger of permanent brain damage.

Other unpleasant effects of the major tranquillizers include dizziness, dry mouth, constipation, blurring of vision, headaches and depression. Uncommon hazards include inflammation of the liver, skin allergies and, rarely, upsets of the blood-forming tissues in the bone-marrow, which may be fatal.

From this catalogue of the unpleasant side-effects of the major tranquillizers it might appear unjustifiable to use them under any circumstances. But schizophrenia is often so serious an illness that the benefits of these drugs in controlling the more severe symptoms outweigh the dangers. However, the diagnosis of schizophrenia must be unequivocal or the disturbed behaviour gross; the major tranquillizers should not be used in high dosage unnecessarily. When psychiatrists prescribe major tranquillizers in high dosage, they are usually careful to administer appropriate antidotes for the extrapyramidal effects. The Soviet psychiatrists have been accused of administering powerful major tranquillizers in high dosage for long periods of time without taking measures to minimize the side-effects. Such a practice is inhumane and would lead one to suspect that the drugs are primarily punishment, not treatment.

Similarly, the notorious sulphazin 'treatment' is presumably given as a punishment, since any therapeutic effect in schizophrenia is unproven. The 'treatment' consists of injections of the drug which acts as a pyrogen – that is, it causes fever. In addition, the injections are painful and stomach cramps occur. Sulphazin injections were used long ago in some countries to treat patients with general paralysis (a form of syphilis) but have been superseded by penicillin. Its use in schizophrenia is quite unjustified.

The use of insulin in the treatment of schizophrenia is also generally considered obsolete, as any improvement following the insulin-induced coma was shown to be due to the intensive nursing of the patient and not to a specific effect of insulin. Again, the treatments are unpleasant and their continuing use, as reported by various dissidents, does not increase one's faith in either the medical or the moral expertise of the Soviet psychiatrists in the special hospitals.

Release

When ordering compulsory psychiatric treatment, the court imposes no time limit on the detention: release depends on the patient regaining his sanity. Every patient must be reviewed by a psychiatric commission every six months. The commission invariably examines the political or religious dissident from the original standpoint, namely, whether he still holds his minority views. If the individual refuses to recant, protests at his forcible detention and treatment, and complains of hospital conditions, he is re-affirmed as mentally ill.

Many dissidents have refused to renounce their views and have remained incarcerated for several years. Others realized that their only hope of release involved persuading the psychiatric commission that they had renounced their dissent. Mr Bukovsky and Dr Gluzman in the *Manual on Psychiatry for Dissidents* specifically advise dissidents to confide to their doctors that former unhealthy convictions have been reappraised.

The psychiatric commission's findings are conveyed to the court and may consist of a recommendation for release, transfer to an ordinary mental hospital or continued confinement in the special hospital. However, even if the psychiatrists now find the patient sane, the recommendation for release may be rejected by the court, often at the instigation of the Procurator. For example, in 1969 Victor Kuznetsov, arrested for possessing *samizdat,* was found insane and committed to Kazan special psychiatric hospital. In November 1970 he was deemed sane and fit for release by a psychiatric commission. However, this advice was refused by the court because the Procurator insisted that Kuznetsov's captivity be prolonged 'in view of the gravity of his guilt'. Other examples have been documented.

This action establishes beyond any lingering doubt that psychiatry is abused in the Soviet Union. Such decisions prove incontrovertibly that the real purpose of referring dissenters to psychiatric commissions is not just to unmask their views as lunatic but, more important, to punish them without compassion. The Soviet authorities seize the opportunity to have their political opponents judged insane and not responsible for their actions, but then castigate them as if they were responsible.

Nevertheless, dissidents *are* released from psychiatric hospitals, usually when they have been locked away for about the time they would have served in the ordinary prison camps. Grigorenko, Borisov, and Gershuni have been set free; Fainberg, Gorbenskaya, Plyushch and Bukovsky have been expelled from the Soviet Union. In their place, other dissidents are being subjected to the same oppression – arrest, finding of unfitness to plead and imprisonment in psychiatric Gehennas.

Overview

No Western psychiatrist reading the available material can state *categorically* that the political and religious dissidents were not suffering from mental illnesses. However, nothing in any of the case-histories is suggestive of *definite* mental illness. The 'symptoms' advanced by the Soviet psychiatrists as evidence of 'creeping schizophrenia' or 'paranoid development of the personality' reflect the content of the patients' beliefs and cannot be used as independent evidence of mental derangement. As such 'symptoms' are the only ones provided to support the diagnosis of mental illness and the non-accountability of the dissidents I conclude that political expediency over-rides medical considerations.

CHAPTER 10

The World Psychiatric Association

This chapter considers the reactions of psychiatrists outside the Soviet Union to the allegations of professional misconduct by their Soviet colleagues. Although there have been many individual protests, activity has centred on persuading international bodies to investigate and, if necessary, to intervene. With improvements in communications the twentieth century has seen the establishment of many organizations which attempt to represent common interests. In psychiatry the international body is the World Psychiatric Association. However, as in all such bodies, the strength may lie in the membership but the activity rests with the executive body to which the membership entrusts the day-to-day management of affairs. Where the executive body is international in its representation and geographically dispersed, the power tends to concentrate in the hands of one or other member of the executive. The entire reputation of that body then depends on the attitudes and biases of that one man. It is an onerous responsibility, especially when, as in this case, politics have intruded on professional matters. Whether that responsibility has been fully and fairly discharged in the W.P.A. must be left to the reader to decide.

Like many international professional organizations, the W.P.A. is designed to further common interests rather than to censure member societies or even to encourage open discussion. It evolved from the Society for the Holding of World Congresses of Psychiatry. Founded in 1961, the W.P.A. is an Association of National Societies of Psychiatry and currently comprises about seventy-five member societies, representing over 60,000 psychiatrists. Two thirds of these psychiatrists practise either in the U.S.S.R. or in the U.S.A.

As laid down in the Statutes, the purpose of the W.P.A. is to 'advance international cooperation in the field of psychiatry by co-ordinating on a world-wide basis the activities of its Member Associations and in other ways to promote activities designed to lead to increased knowledge in the field of mental illness and better care for the mentally ill.'

The governing body of the W.P.A., the General Assembly, is composed of the delegates of member societies and the members of the full Committee and the Executive Committee. The General Assembly convenes about once every six years, on the occasion of each World Psychiatric Congress. The Committee is elected by the General Assembly and totals twenty-four members representing various nations and different psychiatric viewpoints; it is advisory, having few powers, and meets about once every three years.

The actual power is vested in the Executive Committee, in particular in its Secretary General, who manages the secretariat and thus controls every function of the W.P.A. The Executive Committee comprises the President, Vice-President and two Associate Secretaries, who are all elected by the General Assembly; their term of office is the period between two Congresses, normally five to six years. The Secretary General and the Treasurer, who, for administrative convenience, must live in the same country, are appointed for two such periods, that is, ten to twelve years. The Secretary General is responsible for effecting all the decisions of the General Assembly. He convenes the Executive Committee about every six months.

The Secretariat is located in an office in the Maudsley Hospital, Camberwell, South-East London, the place of work of Denis Leigh, the Secretary General. Two or three multilingual secretaries deal with the voluminous correspondence from member societies and individual psychiatrists throughout the world. About six advisers (psychiatrists recruited by the Secretary General and endorsed by the Executive Committee) help with W.P.A. activities, such as publicity or, in my case, scientific meetings (symposia).

The W.P.A. is financed by subscriptions from the member societies and profits from the World Congresses of Psychiatry. By careful husbanding of resources it has attained financial stability.

The most important *executive* member of the Executive Committee is not the President but the Secretary General. He can take initiatives or suppress matters because he controls incoming information, the agenda for committee meetings, and so on. The President has a prestigious position and chairs Committee meetings but would find difficulty in acting independently of the Secretary General, since he has no ready access to the Secretariat. Indeed he may live in another continent.

Denis Leigh was elected Secretary General at the Madrid Congress in 1966 and holds office until the Congress in Honolulu in 1977. Born in 1915, he qualified in medicine at Manchester University in 1939 and is a consultant psychiatrist at the Maudsley Hospital. He is complex, sometimes to the point of paradox. A bluff North-Countryman, authoritarian in outlook, he does not shrink from telling those in authority the shortcomings of their psychiatric services. Usually very sure of himself, he may nevertheless be indecisive and seek the advice of men less able than himself. He declares that he does not suffer fools gladly, yet he tolerates them with only a tinge of acerbity. He delegates responsibility but watches warily until thoroughly convinced of his assistant's competence. Immensely hard-working and full of schemes and initiatives, he is sometimes slow to admit the impracticality of his more extravagant ideas. He reckons himself an internationalist, and indeed young acolytes from all over the world come to him for training. He behaves towards them as the Great Sahib distributing largesse to the natives (he was in India during the War); with few exceptions ex-pupils remember him with affection, gratitude and perhaps a modicum of tolerant amusement. Although I disappointed him by resigning from the W.P.A. at an inopportune time, there is no rancour between us. I have no doubt that psychiatrists throughout the world are indebted to Denis Leigh for his advancement of the W.P.A. into an efficient professional organization to represent their common interests and into a forum for scientific and medical discussion.

He has maintained doggedly that the W.P.A. has no political function and, according to the letter of its statutes, he is right. But was this sufficient? His actions in ethical and political matters impinging on psychiatry are set out later in this chapter. The later years of his tenure of office have been overshadowed by such issues.

The Treasurer, Professor Linford Rees (at present President of the Royal College of Psychiatrists), is an affable, urbane, avuncular Welshman. He is a busy member of the medical establishment in Great Britain, sitting on many government committees. Professor Linford Rees is usually prepared to accept the compromise solution when a less conciliatory person would have taken a more extreme, inflexible line.

The President elected in 1966 was Professor J. J. López Ibor, Professor of Psychiatry and Psychology in Madrid. A firm supporter of General Franco, Professor López Ibor is said to be a personal adviser to Prince (now King) Juan Carlos. An erudite and able psychiatrist, Professor López Ibor has numerous offspring, some of them employed in the family enterprise, a large private psychiatric clinic in Madrid.

The Vice-President was Professor W. von Baeyer, an elderly, aristocratic German psychiatrist with a conscience. He researched on the mental health of the survivors of Nazi concentration camps. The other two Executive Committee members were Professor Carlos León from Colombia, who attended infrequently because of travel problems, and Professor Harvey J. Tompkins, a New York psychiatrist immersed in American medical administration and politics.

Events up to the World Congress, 1971

The first letter about the abuse of psychiatry in the Soviet Union was received by the W.P.A. in August 1970. Denis Leigh states that he raised the matter informally with Soviet psychiatrists, presumably Professors Snezhnevsky and Vartanian, during the W.P.A. symposium in Leningrad in September 1970. However, the problem was not discussed formally at the Executive Committee meeting held then, nor at the following one, in May 1971 in Washington. By 1971 several letters had been received from concerned doctors and laypeople, both in the U.K. and abroad, and Denis Leigh states that the matter was in fact considered at the Washington Executive Committee meeting. Perhaps it was not discussed formally enough to minute.

As the file of correspondence grew, Dr Leigh decided to transmit a copy of this file to Professor Snezhnevsky, the representative of the Soviet All-Union Society of Psychiatrists. A letter denying the charges was sent back within two weeks.

By mid-1971 it was generally known that a World Congress of Psychiatry was scheduled in Mexico City at the end of November. For example, Vladimir Bukovsky, when sending relevant documents, including case-histories, to the West, urged that the topic be fully aired at that Congress. On 16 September 1971 a group of distinguished psychiatrists led by Professor F. A. Jenner of Sheffield wrote to *The Times* highlighting the problem and calling on their colleagues throughout the world to raise the issue at the Congress. Among the signatories was Professor von Baeyer, the Vice-President.

As well as this pressure from individuals, there had already been an official move. On 19 January 1971 the Board of Directors of the Canadian Psychiatric Association expressed concern 'regarding the alleged wrongful detention in mental hospitals in the USSR of seemingly healthy individuals whose views and attitudes are in conflict with those of the regime.' They urged the Canadian Medical Association to scrutinize the evidence and to press strongly for further study and action through various organizations, including the W.P.A. In due course a communication was received by the W.P.A. secretariat in London and was presumably transmitted to Moscow with the rest of the file.

The World Congress, 1971

When the Executive Committee met on 27 November 1971 in Mexico City Denis Leigh reported that a number of complaints had been received from *individuals* and forwarded to Professor Snezhnevsky in Moscow. This was approved, although Professor von Baeyer in a moving emotional appeal urged real action. Dr Leigh explained that he had explored the possibility of appointing an Ethical Committee to consider the issue. He had corresponded with the United Nations Commission on Human Rights, the World Health Organization, the Council of Europe and its Commission of Human Rights, the Council for International Organizations of Medical Sciences, and through it UNESCO and the World Medical Association. These august bodies agreed that an Ethical Committee might be appropriate, but carefully avoided comment on the allegations themselves.

The Committee of the W.P.A., meeting the next day, heard Denis Leigh recount his activities with respect to the allegations. He circulated a document in which he pointed out, quite correctly, that the Statutes contain no reference to the W.P.A.'s being responsible for the ethical aspects of psychiatry, nor was there any mechanism for dealing with complaints by one member society against another. Further, he stated, no member society had complained against another; all complaints had been made by individuals. Legalistically speaking, Dr Leigh was, and is, right. But surely an international society like the W.P.A. has general responsibilities not detailed by its founding fathers?

On 29 November the General Assembly met, but the allegations were not on the agenda. However, such was the activity behind the scenes that pressure mounted for the matter to be discussed. Despite Russian opposition, when the General Assembly was reconvened on 1 December amid intensified concern, this item was on the agenda. Professor López Ibor outlined the steps taken by the Secretary General and suggested that the institution of an Ethical Committee might be advisable. But even this temporizing manoeuvre was unacceptable to the Communist psychiatrists. The Czechoslovak representative in a panic-stricken speech vehemently opposed the setting up of this Committee without consultation among the member societies. Various delegates supported the proposal, others opposed it.

Denis Leigh writes (*British Medical Journal*, 30 August 1975) that the General Assembly 'unanimously rejected' the proposal. However, the minutes clearly state that the proposal to set up the Ethical Committee was to be postponed and, on the suggestion of Professor Tompkins, referred back to the Executive Committee. As the Executive Committee is the ruling body of the W.P.A. between World Congresses, it could have taken any necessary measures on its own initiative. That it did not do so immediately was partly due to its new membership.

The New Executive Committee

The newly-elected President was Howard Rome, Head of Psychiatry at the Mayo Clinic in the United States. He is a quiet, courteous, friendly man; his main previous interest was the mental health policies of the U.S.A. The Vice-President, a Mexican psychiatrist, Professor Ramón de la Fuente, is undoubtedly concerned about the abuse of psychiatry in the U.S.S.R. Unfortunately he has been very preoccupied with problems in his own university and has been unable to attend some of the Executive Committee meetings.

One Associate Secretary is Professor Tolani Asuni of Nigeria, a Dublin graduate and an old friend of Denis Leigh's. He has argued repeatedly for more activity by the W.P.A. in preventing abuses of psychiatry.

He is, however, outweighed by the other Associate Secretary, Professor Marat Vartanian, a huge, affable Armenian in his mid-forties. Professor Vartanian is a trained psychiatrist and had a responsible post in Armenia before becoming Chief of the Laboratory of General Pathophysiology in Professor Snezhnevsky's Institute. Professor Vartanian's research is highly technical but involves schizophrenics, so that he is fully cognizant of the issues. He is well-dressed, travels freely in the West, and has been named as a member of the K.G.B., which he denies. I accept his denial, but he may well hold high rank in the Communist Party and he is probably close to people with real power. He is a superb apologist for his country and its politico-economic system and is well aware of its problems. He speaks good English and is by far the most sophisticated Russian of my acquaintance. He has repeatedly rebutted the allegations against the Russian psychiatrists.

Events up to the Russian Visit in 1973

The neophytes on the Executive Committee were even more swayed by Denis Leigh, with his six years' experience of international medical politics.

At the first meeting of the new Executive Committee in May 1972 in Madrid, Denis Leigh reported the receipt of a letter from the President of the American Psychiatric Association containing a position statement: 'The American Psychiatric Association firmly opposes the misuse of psychiatric facilities for the detention of persons solely on the basis of their political dissent, no matter where it occurs.' It was agreed to circulate this letter to the Executive Committee for consideration at the next meeting in six months' time.

In November 1972 in London, there was a full discussion but little zeal for any strong positive moves by the W.P.A. Professor Vartanian argued that political problems were not the responsibility of the W.P.A. and that the Executive Committee should not proceed with the discussion. The view was also expressed that the formulation of ethical principles was too formidable an undertaking for the W.P.A. with its limited resources. Thus the specific problem of the allegations of the abuse of psychiatry in the U.S.S.R. was engulfed in the morass of general ethical questions. Nevertheless, it was agreed to circulate the position statement of the A.P.A. to the other member societies.

At the European Symposium held at that time, the protests by both medical and lay-people continued. A demonstration was mounted outside the premises of the Royal College of Physicians, opposite Regent's Park, where the Symposium was being held. Simultaneously a telegram was received by Denis Leigh, from, I think, a group of concerned people in France, requesting the W.P.A.'s intervention on behalf of Dr Semyon Gluzman in Kiev. Professor Vartanian denied knowledge of both Dr Gluzman and the prison sentence but promised to make inquiries.

In 1973 it became generally known that the W.P.A. was organizing a Symposium on Schizophrenia in the Soviet Union in conjunction with the Russian psychiatrists. As well as the W.P.A. Executive Committee, the President of the American Psychiatric Association had been invited, and distinguished research and academic psychiatrists from many European countries were on the programme. Among the British contingent were Professor John Wing, a world expert on the social aspects of psychiatry, in particular schizophrenia, and myself, as Symposium Adviser but also invited to summarize the research of my team on the use of tranquillizers in schizophrenia.

I received letters from many private individuals and from groups such as the Ukrainian exiles. Most vilified me for agreeing to go to the U.S.S.R., claiming that my attendance would be exploited as a sign of acquiescence in the obnoxious abuses. Other letters more reasonably urged me to keep an open mind; yet others, from individuals whose political persuasion was patent, confided that on my return I would certainly feel able to vindicate the good name of the U.S.S.R.

Zhores Medvedev rescued me from my dilemma. He had come to the United Kingdom to work for a time at the National Institute for Medical Research in Mill Hill, London. Soon his Soviet passport was revoked and he became an exile. At the height of the furore, he wrote to the prestigious scientific periodical *Nature* (24 August 1973): 'I do not want foreign psychiatrists to boycott this meeting. But I hope very much that ... Western scientists will ask their Soviet colleagues a few specific questions.' He then listed questions relating to several aspects of the detention of political dissidents in special mental hospitals.

John Wing and I decided to meet Dr Medvedev to ask him to elaborate on his questions, to provide us with information on the Soviet legal system, and to amplify some details of his own forced detention in Kaluga mental hospital. I learnt much at this meeting; in particular, the assertion that the Soviet authorities were *systematically* referring dissidents for psychiatric assessment seemed well-founded. The way in which the accused forfeited his civil rights when found unfit to plead, the impotence of the defence counsel, the lack of appeal procedures and the power of the Procuracy were fully discussed. I concluded that the W.P.A. had handled the allegations too ineptly and that the Soviet authorities, political and psychiatric, could not expect their monotonous denials of such well-substantiated allegations to be believed without providing some counter-evidence.

The Symposium in the Caucasus, 1973

On Friday, 5 October, I flew to Moscow. I was met at Sheremetievo Airport by a young Russian psychiatrist who told me that the All-Union Society of Psychiatrists had organized a one-day meeting at the Serbsky Institute to discuss the problem fully. With dismay I learnt that the date suggested was 15

October, three days after the symposium finished in the Caucasus; I had a long-standing firm commitment to fly on to Yugoslavia on 14 October to examine a candidate for a higher degree. The problems of postponing my trip to Yugoslavia now that I was already in the U.S.S.R. proved insurmountable, and I realized I would miss the opportunity to discuss case-histories with my Russian colleagues.

On Monday, 8 October, the W.P.A. Executive met in Yerevan in Armenia, and was told by Denis Leigh of his meeting with the Soviet Deputy Minister of Health, Dr Dimitri Venedictov, on 5 October. The Minister had welcomed the action of the Soviet psychiatrists in arranging the meeting at the Serbsky, because they could then prove to their Western colleagues that they had behaved ethically and professionally. I was told later that Dr Venedictov had opposed the meeting, and the Soviet psychiatric establishment, Professor Snezhnevsky in particular, had pleaded for permission to hold it. Denis Leigh had informed the Minister that the W.P.A. Executive Committee would attend the meeting not in their official capacity but as individuals.

The Executive Committee welcomed the chance to visit the Serbsky, but Dr Alfred Freedman, the President of the American Psychiatric Association, was less easily convinced. What could be achieved in so short a time? None of the Westerners spoke Russian, most were not forensic experts. Would there be a press conference, and how would it be reported in the Soviet Union?

Despite these disquieting comments the Executive Committee conveyed to the twenty-five or so overseas visitors the Soviet psychiatrists' invitation to attend 'a full and free professional discussion on the alleged abuse of psychiatry in the Soviet Union'. Already tensions were heightening. News of the Arab-Israeli Yom Kippur War, which had started on 6 October, had reached us via the American Embassy and the newspaper reporters accompanying us in Soviet Armenia. If the conflict escalated, our status as honoured guests might be imperilled.

The invitation to the Serbsky meeting immediately cast an additional onus on those able to attend.

The Western psychiatrists divided into three groups. One consisted of those ill-informed about the details of the problem who were being dragooned rather unwillingly into the political arena. The 'hard-liners' were convinced that the Soviet authorities would merely make political capital out of a visit which would be stage-managed to prevent any informed judgement. The Soviet authorities, they said, would exploit the presence of the Western psychiatrists as evidence, at least for internal consumption, confirming the probity of Soviet psychiatry – 'a Red whitewash'. The third group were curious to hear the Soviet version of events and were less uneasy about the Soviet authorities' future propaganda.

I believed that in the matter of internal news the authorities would profit either way. If we went, they would claim that we had approved their activities; if we stayed away, they would assert that the allegations were Western propaganda fabrications which had led us to prejudge the issue. The Russian authorities completely controlled their own news media; but if we went we could at least inform the Western press of our impressions.

Various meetings took place among the Western psychiatrists. Deputations negotiated with the Russians, mainly over two conditions: first, that the visit could not in itself be construed as acceptance or rejection of any of the allegations; secondly, that, since the complex issues raised could not be resolved in a one-day meeting, we wished to begin a continuing dialogue. The Russians baulked at these conditions, but the overseas visitors made it clear that these were the principles guiding their own participation in the Serbsky meeting. The negotiations with the Russians were with Professors Vartanian and Snezhnevsky, although the importance apparently given to this visit was evidenced by Minister Venedictov joining us at one point.

During the second half of the Symposium in Tbilisi, a

curious incident occurred. At one of the sessions a man tried to address the meeting, but was escorted out by Professor Zurabashvili, the doyen of Georgian psychiatrists. That evening the man was examined by Doctors de la Fuente, Leigh and Linford Rees at the Asatiani Institute of Psychiatry of the Georgian Ministry of Health. It transpired that the man had been mentally ill for many years, that he was a voluntary patient in a mental hospital and had no complaints about his treatment.

Despite the hospitality – I cannot recall who were the more overwhelming, the Armenians or the Georgians – I was relieved to leave Russia to fly to Belgrade.

The Meeting at the Serbsky

I am grateful to my colleagues, in particular John Wing, for the following account.

On Monday, 15 October, thirteen psychiatrists from Western countries, including four members of the Executive Committee (Linford Rees had returned to the U.K.), attended the meeting at the Serbsky. Almost immediately Denis Leigh and Carlo Perris, a Swedish psychiatrist, accompanied by two Russian psychiatrists, travelled to see Major-General Grigorenko in Hospital No. 5, forty miles from Moscow. General Grigorenko refused to be examined by foreign psychiatrists except in the presence of an interpreter approved by his wife. This sensible precaution against misrepresentation by an official interpreter illustrates the problems faced by any non-Russian-speaking delegation of Western psychiatrists.

At the Serbsky, the first two hours were devoted to general items about the law in relation to psychiatry. Next, the case-histories of five dissidents were presented and questions answered. This was most informative, as some of these case-histories were among those sent out by Mr Bukovsky to the West. Thus, the clinical data available to Western psychiatrists could be validated against the best possible source, the

Soviet psychiatrists' own case-notes. As far as can be ascertained, those case-histories that could be checked were essentially the same, though with some differences in emphasis. The authenticity is also established in reverse: the Russian psychiatrists presented material by and large vouched for by some of the dissidents themselves.

No elements of the case-histories presented at the Serbsky adequately supported the Soviet contention that the dissidents were insane and devoid of responsibility. When pressed to list the features leading to their diagnoses of schizophrenia, the Soviet psychiatrists echoed the well-worn phrases 'reformist delusions', 'moralizing', 'undue self-esteem'. Thus psychiatrists unwilling to support the diagnosis of schizophrenia on the basis of the material available in the West were most unlikely to have this reluctance dispelled by the evidence presented at the Serbsky.

The Aftermath

The W.P.A. Executive Committee reconvened that evening and approved a Press statement which 'expressed their satisfaction with the frank and friendly atmosphere in which the meeting had taken place'. Professor Vartanian dissented from the exclusion of the following sentence included in the draft statement: 'All five cases had suffered from a mental illness at the time of their respective Commissions of Enquiry.'

By contrast, several Western psychiatrists who attended the Serbsky meeting stated afterwards that they did not think that the dissidents whose case-summaries they heard were 'insane', that is, non-imputable. The comments of Professors Freedman and Wing were reported widely in Western newspapers.

My own connection with the W.P.A. was severed soon after these events. My inquiries before I went to the Soviet Union, the unsatisfactory answers of the Soviet psychiatrists to my queries about legal procedure, the account of the Serbsky meeting and my contacts with a few Russian psychiatrists unhappy with the situation all led me to conclude that the allegations of abuse of psychiatry in the Soviet Union had some foundation. I gave an interview to John Stevenson, science correspondent of the *Daily Mail*, in which I stated unambiguously that Russian political dissidents were being diagnosed as schizophrenics on criteria unacceptable in Britain. When the newspaper article was published, Denis Leigh rightly asked me to resign from the W.P.A., since he regarded such a public statement as incompatible with my position as Symposium Adviser to an organization containing the psychiatrists I was criticizing. I resigned immediately.

One immediate outcome of the Tbilisi meeting was that Denis Leigh used the powers given him by the General Assembly at the Mexico City Congress and instituted a working party on ethical matters. It consists of three distinguished Scandinavians, Professor Leo Eitinger of Oslo, Dr Clarence Blomquist of Stockholm, and Dr Gerdt Wretmark of Linkö-ping, Sweden. All three are men of high integrity and are profoundly concerned by the abuse of psychiatry and the exercise of totalitarian power.

Professor Wing wrote an article in the *British Medical Journal* in which he stated clearly that the practice of Soviet psychiatrists in the case of the political dissidents whose histories were summarized at the Serbsky meeting would be found unacceptable in the West. Dr G. Morozov, the Director of the Serbsky Institute, wrote a bland reply, published in the *British Medical Journal* on 6 July 1974, giving his own version of events. The key paragraph reads:

On the basis of this discussion the participants in the conference assessed the professional level and system of psychiatric tests at the Serbsky Institute in a positive light. Those participating in the conference, like the Executive Committee of the World Psychiatric Association, verified that all five of the so-called dissidents, who had previously been acknowledged as irresponsible, were suffering from mental illnesses during the legal examination.

Professor Wing replied pointing out that this statement,

echoing what had been reported in the Soviet press, was untrue.

On 30 August 1975 the *British Medical Journal* published a letter from Denis Leigh rebutting some of the inaccuracies in Dr Morozov's statements. He pointed out that the Executive Committee went to the Serbsky in a personal, non-official capacity, made no official W.P.A. pronouncement and did not comment on the mental state of the individuals whose case-histories were presented. Dr Leigh did not, however, challenge the substance of Morozov's statement that Western psychiatrists had agreed that the dissenters were 'insane'. He apologized for the delay in replying to Dr Morozov's letter, but that was 'due to a number of factors'.

Within the Soviet Union, Dr Morozov could and did claim without rebuff the endorsement of Western psychiatrists for the Serbsky procedures; and the W.P.A. allowed the propaganda potential abroad of this claim to be fully exploited for over a year, in spite of the fact that Wing, Freedman and others had publicly denied it. The delay was unnecessary. At the meeting of the Executive Committee on 10 November 1974, at Professor Asuni's insistence, Dr Leigh was directed to issue a denial of Dr Morozov's letter. Not until an editorial was published in the *British Medical Journal* of 9 August 1975 did Denis Leigh carry out his explicit instructions.

National Psychiatric Associations

Many psychiatric associations, such as the Canadian and the Federal (West) German, have been actively concerned and have officially deplored the Soviet situation. Others have been less outspoken. The American Psychiatric Association approved the position statement mentioned earlier and took steps to bring it to the notice of other national societies. Undoubtedly many American psychiatrists such as Professor Freedman are deeply troubled and have communicated directly with the Russians. One hopes that there is much activity behind the scenes at the American Psychiatric Association.

The Royal College of Psychiatrists has been more active, but it represents far fewer psychiatrists in a country with much less political power. Over the past two or three years several resolutions concerning the abuse of psychiatry have been passed at General Meetings of the College. Initially the resolutions were as unspecific as the American Psychiatric Association's position statement. Later, the motions carried became increasingly censorious.

One particular concern has been the fate of Dr Semyon Gluzman. Professor Sir Martin Roth, the Foundation President of the Royal College, addressed a personal letter to Professor Snezhnevsky inquiring about Dr Gluzman, but he was fobbed off with a denial that Dr Gluzman was a psychiatrist. Professor Roth replied more acidly, pointing out that recent evidence had confirmed the reality of Dr Gluzman's psychiatric training but he received no reply. Following the Annual General Meeting of the College in July 1975, Professor Roth sent the following telegram to Professor Snezhnevsky:

On behalf of the Royal College of Psychiatrists I wish to protest in the strongest terms against the continued incarceration of Gluzman, Bukovsky and Plyushch which appears a perversion of psychiatric practice and denial of natural justice. Your refusal to take action or to respond constitutes a slur on our profession.

Further motions were proposed at later College meetings, stinging Professor Snezhnevsky into a pained and petulant reply. He invoked the Helsinki declaration establishing 'peaceful relations between countries', 'discrepant opinions' in international diagnostic practice, and accused the Royal College of 'using mentally ill patients for political purposes'. Perhaps he believes the College to have reformist delusions.

Professor Roth has been deeply and consistently worried about the problem and took many initiatives on behalf of the College. His term of office finished in 1975 and he was succeeded by Professor Linford Rees, who has punctiliously carried out the College's wishes in this matter. However, as he is also Treasurer of the W.P.A., he has undoubted conflicts of interest and could not be expected to initiate moves of censure against another member society of the W.P.A. Might such censure moves be instigated by the Royal College at the next World Congress of Psychiatry in August 1977?

CHAPTER 11

What Is To Be Done?

The psychiatric detention of political dissidents in the U.S.S.R. is not new. During Stalinist times some prisoners had their lives saved by being deemed insane by psychiatrists. But the practice continued after Stalin's death and was investigated in 1955–6 on the instigation of Party member S. P. Pisarev. A special commission reported that abuses of psychiatry had been perpetrated 'year after year', in particular at the Serbsky Institute by Dr D. R. Lunts. *Plus ça change* . . . This officially sponsored report was suppressed. In 1962 the Soviet writer Valery Tarsis was arrested and confined in a Moscow psychiatric hospital, an experience related in his book *Ward 7*. By the mid-1960s several dissidents whose names are now well-known in the West (Bukovsky, Grigorenko, Yesenin-Volpin) had already been in these notorious prison hospitals. However, it was the forced detention of Dr Medvedev which sparked off a continuing concern and a mounting sense of outrage in the West.

If the Soviets are to be deterred from abusing psychiatry, objectives must be clearly defined, the decision to confront or persuade the Russians taken, the appropriate individuals and organizations mobilized and the consequences of such pressure evaluated.

What Needs To Be Done?

The Political Offence

If there were no political or religious dissenters, or if the authorities were tolerant of these people, the problem would vanish. The aim of the Soviet authorities is to stifle dissent not by abolishing the grounds for complaint but by removing the complainers. Over the past couple of years repression of dissent has intensified, so that freedom is threatened more than at any time since Stalin's death. No hope for improvement is apparent; Soviet attitudes and practices towards dissent are extremely harsh, rigid, vindictive and unforgiving by Western democratic standards.

Dissent is a disarticulated movement among an infinitesimal minority. By and large the Soviet people support their government. The Communist Party's modernization programme produced rapid industrialization, social mobility, political awareness, and impressive achievements in science, education and public health. In spite of hardships, frustrations and an economy effectively on a war footing, material progress has been substantial. The grumbles are perennial, but the average Russian prefers the authorities he knows to the uncertainties of a democratic government.

Thus schemes to incite the Russian people to overthrow the regime are futile: no reservoirs of popular democratic sentiment are available to be undammed. Submission is deeply etched into the Russian character, not only from self-preservation in Stalinist times but from pre-revolutionary Russian tradition. The peoples of the Communist satellites are less tractable, as are such Soviet minorities as the Crimean Tatars, the Baptists and the world's most contumacious minority, the Jews. The *status quo* serves the interests of the elite as well as the peasant, the intelligentsia as well as the bureaucracy. Only a handful recognize the advantages of democratization, and even then most seek to reform the system from within. The authorities interpret dissent as incompatible with the optimal functioning of the system. Their obsession with suppressing dissent is a neurotic over-reaction, not a psychotic paranoia as with Stalin and Hitler. Neurotic reactions tend to be chronic and fluctuating in course, but they often respond to group therapy; perhaps Soviet Russia will overcome her caution and suspicion, and in joining the comity of nations will be influenced by the moral attitudes of the Western democracies.

Another more tangible hope lies in the advance of science and technology. Many Soviet scientists have realized that more contact with the West strengthens their own scientific endeavours. Further, an advanced technological society must be politically modern, flexible and responsive.

Those irreconcilable to Soviet Russia are on the horns of a dilemma. If they strive to lessen the objectionable features of the regime, they improve it and thereby strengthen it; if they impugn it directly, they provide the Soviet authorities with proof of external animosity which also bolsters up the regime. Similarly, people urging reform can take a short- or long-term view: but the short-term tactic of exerting pressure to ameliorate conditions for dissidents increases the suspicion of the Soviet peoples; the alternative strategy of allaying distrust by reasoned discussion does little immediately for the prisoners.

Thus it is futile to believe that the Soviet government can be forced to liberalize soon and fast. Dissenters, political and religious, will continue to be arrested and tried and to need help.

Referral for Psychiatric Examination

Amnesty International has made several recommendations, with which I agree. They urge that Soviet legislation be revised in several respects:

1. Article 46 of the Code of Criminal Procedure guarantees the right of an accused person to know what he is accused of and to give explanations concerning the accusations; to present evidence; to submit petitions; to become acquainted with the materials of the case; to have defence counsel; to submit challenges; and to appeal against the actions and decisions of the investigators, Procurator and court.

All these rights of the accused should be preserved for accused persons whose mental health is questioned.

2. At every step the accused should be kept informed of the

legal and medical measures instituted. In particular he should be informed, whether it is believed he can understand the information or not, when it has been decided to refer him to a forensic psychiatric commission.

3. Such an accused person should be guaranteed access to a lawyer of his own or his family's choice and regular communication with his friends and family.

4. The accused should be allowed access to a defence counsel from the time he is referred for examination and not merely after his mental illness has been established by the psychiatric commission. At present he is bereft of advice at this crucial time.

5. The accused should be allowed to nominate a member of the psychiatric commission and to object to the inclusion of a member he believes inimical.

6. The accused should be present during the fact-finding of the commission and have the right to question and challenge the examining psychiatrists.

Nevertheless, humanitarian administration of the law is more important than jurists' clauses, especially as many existing rights and safeguards are imperfectly implemented. The paternalism of the Soviet system should be recognized as having outlived its usefulness. The court should steer between the Scylla of over-protective deprivation of basic human rights and the Charybdis of subjecting the mentally ill to further distress.

The Diagnosis

Moscow psychiatrists apparently use wide concepts of schizophrenia and paranoid personality. As I have repeatedly emphasized, one cannot prove the rightness or wrongness of the diagnosis of these mental conditions, only whether the criteria are generally acknowledged throughout the world or are local idiosyncrasies. The World Health Organization Diagnostic Project's identification of broad concepts in Moscow and in Washington should be confirmed in further studies. Meanwhile, our

183

concern should focus on the circular diagnosis of mental illness based solely on beliefs which initially led to the arrest.
'Reformist ideas', 'moralizing' and 'exaggerated self-import-
ance' should not be deemed sufficient for a diagnosis of
schizophrenia in the absence of other features. Paranoid personality is a vague diagnosis at best and is especially contentious when the implications are so grave. Since it is a
personality abnormality, its boundary with normality is entirely a matter of opinion.

Fitness to Plead

Labelling a dissident mentally abnormal may furnish an excuse for discrediting him, but declaring him unfit to plead or
non-responsible effectively deprives him of his rights. The
inflexibility of Soviet forensic psychiatry results in the diagnosis of schizophrenia being associated with a finding of non-
responsibility in almost all cases. The diagnosis of paranoid
personality also has this consequence with political and religious dissidents. The concept of 'diminished responsibility'
should be commended to the Soviet jurists and forensic psychiatrists for their consideration. Further, the Soviet authorities should be made aware that equating schizophrenia with
non-responsibility and incompetence is an excessively paternalistic stance.

The defendant should have the right of appeal against the
diagnostic findings of the forensic commission and separately
against the juridical findings, namely, unfitness to plead. On
both counts, appeal to a second psychiatric commission
should be facilitated and should not be dependent on the
Procuracy.

Court Appearance

This should be public and the accused allowed to appear. The
court proceedings should be held in his absence only when he
is demonstrably violent or greatly distressed. Even then his
written statements should be admissible in evidence, and his

family and a lawyer of his choice should be in court through-out the proceedings. Court proceedings should never be *in camera*.

All evidence, including the detailed case-notes used by the psychiatric commission, should be available to the defendant, his relatives and counsel. The findings of any independent psychiatric examination should be allowed as evidence.

Sentencing

The defendant should be sent to a special (maximum security) psychiatric institution only when he is a *physical* danger to himself or to others and not because of any *social* danger detected by the court. The inhumaneness of this over-reaction by the authorities should be pointed out. The option of trans-ferring defendants found mentally ill to the guardianship of relatives should be used more often.

Conditions in Hospital

As in many parts of the world, conditions in many Soviet mental hospitals are grossly unsatisfactory. The special insti-tutions in the U.S.S.R. seem egregious, and improvements in basic living conditions are urgently needed.

On the legal side, patients should be informed of their rights. The patient or his family should have the right of appeal to an authority independent of the hospital. The Pro-curacy should be strengthened so it can intercede for the patient. The patient's family, friends and legal representative should be guaranteed regular, reasonable access to him.

The medical and nursing staff of the special psychiatric institutions should take stock of themselves. If they believe they treat patients, any disciplinary measures should be mild, while help and support remain freely available. The present custodial and punitive attitudes of the staff are a discredit to psychiatry. Prisoners in labour colonies have more rights and are punished less capriciously than 'patients' in these hospitals. The Procuracy should be especially concerned about these institutions.

Treatment

The patient and his friends and relatives should have a decisive say in the choice and the application of therapy. The psychiatrist should consult with patients or their families and discuss the goals, advantages and drawbacks of the proposed treatment. Other doctors and psychiatrists, both within and without the institution, should be accessible to advise families about the appropriateness, advisability and dangers of treatment.

Compulsory treatment should be applied only with the consent of an independent panel composed of both doctors and laymen. Response to any compulsory treatment should be carefully and frequently monitored.

Patients and their families should have legal redress against psychiatrists or any other hospital employees whom they believe to have abused their authority. In particular, physical maltreatment of patients, excessive or obsolescent medication, and administrative obstruction of complaints should be subject to careful legal scrutiny.

Review Procedure

The regular six-monthly review of mentally ill persons in special institutions is commendable, but, like the original forensic psychiatric examination, it needs further safeguards. The patient should be informed of the purpose of the examination and of its findings. He should have the right of representation by counsel, his family or friends, and be able to appeal against the commission's conclusions. The recommendations of the commission should be acted on by the Procuracy, so that the case is not referred back to court; at present this reinforces the impression that the dissidents are convicted prisoners and not recovered patients.

Release of Individuals

Pressure from the West has apparently produced the release of dissidents such as Leonid Plyushch. These campaigns focus on one individual with the laudable aim of securing his release. However, for every illustrious figure in the limelight, tens and perhaps hundreds in the same predicament linger in the shadows, unknown and neglected. A nice balance should be sought between general aims of lessening abuses by modifying the legal and psychiatric systems, theories and practice and the specific target of releasing the prominent dissidents.

Although all these recommendations refer specifically to the Soviet Union, the general principles of humane treatment apply throughout the world.

Does Pressure Work?

Reasoned logical argument or impassioned appeal has little effect, so that some element of coercion is necessary. Mr Victor Fainberg, confined for five years in mental hospitals, describes clearly and convincingly how the plight of himself and his companions fluctuated according to the intensity of the Western campaign on their behalf. He noted that a 'huge new wave of repression' followed the W.P.A.'s inactivity at the Mexico City Congress, only to subside when the West began a 'new wave of protests'.

Mr Arkady Levin claims further that his friend Leonid Plyushch was ill-treated in order to gauge the depth of Western feeling, the strength of its protests. The K.G.B. aimed to persuade the West to consider the fate of the dissidents as the Soviet Union's internal affair. By this token, the release of Mr Plyushch was a signal victory for Western humanitarian and liberal sentiments, expressed through pressure on the Soviet authorities.

Who Should Do It?

It would be presumptuous for me to dictate to individuals and groups how they should act concerning the Soviet abuse of psychiatry. Some general humanitarian organizations like Amnesty International have extensive experience of effective manoeuvres. Others have been devoting much time and energy to specific aims. Some political bodies, dedicated to over-throwing the Soviet government, are interested in the abuse of psychiatry only as a tactic to discredit the Soviet system.

Psychiatrists

Psychiatrists must be in the vanguard of any attempts to moderate Soviet excesses. I believe strongly that national psychiatric societies throughout the world should realize that abuse of psychiatry in one country, alleged or proven, impedes the practice of psychiatry elsewhere. Censuring Soviet psychiatrists *is* a definite intervention in the internal affairs of a sovereign power but it is a justifiable, indeed essential, one. I approve of the early initiatives by the Canadian Psychiatric Association and the more recent ones by the Royal College of Psychiatrists. Perhaps the American Psychiatric Association will show more concern, especially as it will be host to the next World Congress of Psychiatry.

Criticisms of Soviet psychiatrists by other psychiatrists should be informed and couched in psychiatric terms. Diagnostic criteria and the concept of responsibility should be debated and the Soviet psychiatrists invited to comment on practice in other countries. All psychiatric systems are imperfect and open to abuse if vigilance is relaxed.

The World Psychiatric Association is not equipped to deal with complaints, but at last it may be taking a less ambiguous and ambivalent attitude. Thus Denis Leigh associated himself and the W.P.A. with a 'message of support and friendship' sent by the Royal College of Psychiatrists to Dr Semyon

Gluzman and, moreover, decided that the W.P.A. should consider the whole question and bring pressure on countries where abuses occur. The W.P.A. may also have made more insistent, informal representations to the Soviet psychiatric and political authorities.

The W.P.A. has two options. It could take the stance that the World Health Organization has adopted throughout, namely, that it is not empowered by its constitution to intervene. Or it could intercede vigorously for those incarcerated in prison mental hospitals, castigate the abusers of psychiatry and risk the Russians' leaving the association. Its member societies must decide their own strategies in influencing the W.P.A., but there is some urgency, as the next appropriate time is the World Congress in Hawaii in August 1977. Some unambiguous proposals for sanctions against transgressors must be tabled for discussion by the General Assembly. Otherwise psychiatrists everywhere will be condemned for their spinelessness.

Laymen

Amnesty International, impatient with the inactivity of the medical profession, held a 'Symposium on the Medical Ethic Faced with Abuses of Psychiatry for Political Purposes' in Geneva in April 1975. The sixty participants unreservedly condemned practices which had recourse to psychiatric treatment 'in violation of human rights, especially if used as a means of repression against religious or political dissenters'. The U.S.S.R. was named specifically. The meeting resolved to create an international organ charged with the task of denouncing and preventing such abuse, having noted that the W.P.A. (and the World Federation for Mental Health, the equivalent lay body) were 'powerless to take the necessary measures'. It is to be hoped that the W.P.A. will give every help.

The Campaign Against Psychiatric Abuses (C.A.P.A.) is the British section of the Initiating Committee against Abuses of

Psychiatry for Political Purposes. Comprising psychiatrists, other doctors, and laymen, it has as its task 'impartially to investigate the abuses of psychiatry whenever and wherever they arise, to condemn and publicise illegal and ethically unjustifiable methods, and to defend those fellow doctors who maintain their professional integrity in spite of police pressures.' It is increasingly active.

Other non-psychiatric bodies include scientists and mathematicians, the latter especially vocal in the cause of Leonid Plyushch. Religious bodies – Catholics, Baptists and Moslems – have taken up the cudgels; American and international Jewish organizations have actively intervened.

The Royal College of Psychiatrists solicited support from the legal profession for a resolution against Soviet abuses of psychiatry. The Secretary of the Bar Council, representing barristers, believed that the Bar would overwhelmingly support such a resolution and would consider taking part in a commission to investigate the problem. The Law Society, representing solicitors, felt unable to participate in order not to compromise its political neutrality.

The general public is most important of all. Professional bodies criticizing parallel organizations in other countries must be supported by their own public opinion. The purpose of this book is to outline the complex issues involved, to provide some background information and to help the informed member of the general public to reach a balanced conclusion.

Pressure on Whom?

One point of influence discussed earlier is that of psychiatrist on psychiatrist. No professional person can easily shrug off accusations of malpractice, inhumanity or indifference from his colleagues. The medical profession derives great support from its supposed favourable public image. Because they traditionally foster a close professional relationship with their patients, psychiatrists are particularly sensitive to insinuations that they are careless of patients' interests or, worse, actually connive with political authorities to degrade and maltreat them. The Soviet psychiatrists, mostly innocent of actively abusing their profession and patients, are all tarred with the same brush as their Serbsky confrères and the M.V.D. psychiatrist-warders in the prison mental hospitals. Pressure on the bulk of Soviet psychiatrists will result in pressure, albeit diffuse and shifting, on their politically accommodating colleagues. Dr Gluzman, martyred by the authorities to demonstrate the fate of dissident psychiatrists, is a special concern.

Expulsion from an international organization like the W.P.A. would dismay the Soviet psychiatrists, especially if the move were backed by psychiatrists from politically uncommitted nations. Soviet Russia is ambivalently eager to join and yet suspicious of international bodies. Expulsion would be denounced as a capitalist plot, but it would injure Soviet scientific prestige. However, expulsion should be the ultimate sanction. In the meantime the W.P.A. should encourage a dialogue between the Soviet psychiatrists and their critics.

The total control of the Russian news media means that Western public opinion has no access either to the policy-makers in the Kremlin or to the Soviet public. Consequently energies are often best guided into an indirect channel. The only people in the West with access to the Soviet leaders are the politicians. Therefore, the most telling way to influence events is to convince our own politicians that while such practices as the abuse of psychiatry continue, any détente or rapprochement can never be more than superficial. Ways of exerting pressure on our own political representatives are well-recognized and need no reiteration.

To be fair, many British politicians have themselves condemned the Soviet abuse of psychiatry, or are sympathetic. For example, when the Royal College of Psychiatrists communicated its indignation to the British government, it received a reply from Mr Roy Hattersley, then Minister of State,

Foreign and Commonwealth, in which he stated that 'Real progress is likely to come through patient discussion and private negotiation rather than through public complaints', and also that 'the Government are prepared to take suitable opportunities to bring to the attention of the Soviet authorities the strength of feeling in this country about certain Soviet domestic policies'.

Politicians' attitudes in the U.S.A. carry great weight because the Soviet Union relies repeatedly on American grain surpluses to compensate for its own shortfalls. If American public opinion became too revolted by the Soviet treatment of dissenters, it might baulk at helping the Soviet economy in this way. Already the U.S. government has been under pressure to make technological aid conditional on the emigration of Soviet Jews. Thus I hope that informed Americans will actively support those seeking to redress the wrongs in the Soviet system and practice and that they will also convey their attitudes to their elected political representatives.

CHAPTER 12

Conclusion: the Implications for Psychiatry

The last five chapters have outlined the totalitarian and intolerant attitudes of the Soviet authorities towards dissent, the 'evidence' that some dissidents are insane and non-imputable, the complex chain of events from crime to punishment, the actions (or lack of them) of official psychiatric bodies, and suggestions for ending the abuse of psychiatry in the Soviet Union. The difficulties in *proving* without doubt that abuse does occur proved great but not insurmountable and are but part of the difficulties of proving anything in psychiatry. The earlier chapters tried to show that psychiatry can be abused because it is a contentious subject still struggling towards scientific and even medical respectability. The brain remains a mysterious organ; few of the secrets of that Pandora's box have so far been revealed. While neurology has reaped much benefit from the development of neurophysiology (the study of brain function), psychiatry has gleaned little of definite relevance.

Events in the mind can be described only with difficulty; the diagnosis of many patients is an arbitrary labelling process; and treatment must be either general common sense and humanity or an unpredictable affair with powerful drugs. The law makes demands of exactitude on the psychiatrist which he is not able to discharge fully, because of the inaccuracies of his subject, yet it invests him with powers of custody over some of his patients. Unlike other doctors, psychiatrists have the role of warder as well as therapist; more than other doctors, psychiatrists have dual professional responsibilities to their patients and to society. In that clash of interests in an inherently weak topic lie the seeds of abuse.

I have been critical and even disparaging about many aspects of psychiatry, but this must not be construed as an anti-psychiatric attitude. However, I *am* anti-humbug. I believe strongly that psychiatry must take three major steps in its own interests which will culminate in a strengthening, not a withering away, of psychiatry. While the human psyche remains imperfect there will be plenty of work for psychiatrists.

The Pretensions

The first step is for psychiatry to return to its legitimate frame of reference with respect both to the psychiatrist and to his patient's health. Some psychiatrists believe that their specialty should sally forth from hospitals, clinics and consulting rooms and seek applications in the concerns of normal people, in national and international affairs, in politics, in race relations and ethnic matters, in government, sport, family life, sexual mores, education and entertainment: in other words that it should busy itself with the optimal performance of human beings as civilized creatures. Psychiatry has already influenced these areas, but often only superficially, contributing phrases to the vernacular like 'sibling rivalry', 'Oedipus complex' and 'Freudian slip'.

Many other psychiatrists view this elongation of psychiatry's tentacles with misgivings or active opposition. They clearly delimit psychiatry to the purview of the traditional physician dealing with patients complaining of symptoms or with social or mental handicap. They have no yearning to remodel the world according to the principles of one or other school of psychiatry. Furthermore, they accept and foster non-medical participation in treatment by encouraging psychologists, nurses, social workers, relatives and others. Because of their ultimate legal responsibility for the patient, they insist on remaining team coordinator, *primus inter pares*.

The general population is also affected by the wide term of

reference proposed by some psychiatrists. 'Health' has been defined by the World Health Organization as 'a state of complete physical, mental, and social well being and not merely the absence of disease or infirmity.' But this is a *reductio ad absurdum*: psychiatrists could use it to claim that anybody not healthy is ill, and since nobody is ever in 'a state of complete physical, mental, and social well being', then everybody is sick.

This is too wide a psychiatric ambit. Many people need help but not necessarily of a medical or psychiatric nature. The treatment of definable mental disease is the province of the psychiatrist; the promotion of well being is his concern but not his responsibility. Coordinated counselling services run by properly trained individuals – financial, legal, social, occupational, educational – should be instituted for those in urgent need who now lack the knowledge, initiative or money to use what is available.

Psychiatry as an Agent of Society

Criticism of psychiatry even in its role of treating symptoms has come from within the profession, linking it to a conformity-imposing society. For example, David Cooper in his book *Psychiatry and Anti-Psychiatry* states the case thus:

Over the last century psychiatry, in the view of an increasing number of present-day psychiatrists, has aligned itself far too closely with the alienated needs of the society within which it functions. In doing so it is perpetually in danger of committing a well-intentioned act of betrayal of those members of society who have been ejected into the psychiatric situation as patients. A great many people today in this country of their own accord go to their doctors seeking psychiatric help. For the most part such people in very practical terms are seeking the gift of a set of techniques that would enable them all the better and more closely to conform with massified social expectations. They are usually assisted towards this goal. A few misguided persons go to the psychiatrist seeking what amounts to a form of spiritual guidance. They are usually rapidly disillusioned.

Thus psychiatry is seen as a well-intentioned but misguided agent of society, imposing conformity on its patients even in symptomatic treatment. But, further, society empowers psychiatrists to deprive certain individuals of their liberty. The usual ground for this legally-sanctioned curtailment of basic human rights is that the patient might endanger himself or others. Most patients admitted to hospital in the U.K. need no coercion, official or unofficial, since some insight is retained. In other cases, relatives and friends recognize the aberrant behaviour and seek help in admitting the patient to hospital. Here, the psychiatrist uses his training and expertise to determine whether to admit the patient or whether the relatives are conniving at 'putting away' the patient for convenience or pecuniary gain.

The ethical problem arises when the patient has lost all insight and has no concerned relatives to safeguard his rights. Grossly abnormal behaviour may indicate to the psychiatrist that the patient suffers a recognized mental malady such as mania or severe depression. Society delegates responsibility to the psychiatrist for ensuring an appropriate balance between the rights of the patient as an individual and the interests of society as his milieu. If the patient recovers fully (as do most manic-depressives) he regains complete insight and with it acknowledges that the restraints, so resented at the time, were in his own interest. But some patients, in particular those with dementia (intellectual decay), do not recuperate and legal detention continues until death.

Consequently some accountability of psychiatrists must be incorporated as a shield against the incompetent, the complacent and the dishonest. Laymen are indispensable members of any supervisory body. Some countries, like the U.K., rely on special commissions, Mental Health Tribunals; others, such as the U.S.A., depend on legal watchdogs. But patients must be apprised of their rights of appeal, and the system must be biased towards too many appeals rather than too few, however irksome that would be for the psychiatrist. Society can legislate appeal procedures but depends on the psychiatrist and his associates to ensure that the machinery is neither sabotaged nor rusty through neglect. In return, society must trust the psychiatrist not to harry his patients into meek compliance. Nor must society expect the psychiatrist to remonstrate with transgressors against the current moral code. The psychiatrist helps solve the medical and social problems of patients as he finds them, not as society wants them to be.

Criticism and Research

Clarifying the relationship between society and psychiatrist is the second step towards the invigoration of psychiatry. The third step is to encourage a process of rationalization by applying to psychiatry the methods of scientific inquiry. As the late Sir Aubrey Lewis, the most critical psychiatrist-savant of this century, said, 'If these [methods] result in encroachments on the area reserved for the art of medicine, and substitute assured knowledge for assumptions and intuitions, so much the better.' While compassion and intuition have a part in psychiatry, they do not lie outside inquiry. Magic and superstition, however, must be exposed and deposed.

Psychiatry is not the only branch of medicine incorporating dogmatism and prejudice. Of course the practitioner has to intervene to the best of his knowledge and abilities to help a patient; neither can wait for elegant scientific research to uncover the causes, mechanisms and cures for mental illness. But in applying his here-and-now remedies, the psychiatrist should not deceive himself and the patient into believing that the psychiatric millennium has already arrived. On the other hand he should not fall back into the bog of therapeutic nihilism which characterized psychiatry in the nineteenth century.

Constructive criticism is the necessary precondition for

advance. It is uncomfortable to have one's presumptions and pretensions laid bare, and critics like myself expect no popularity. But only after rational appraisal can scientific methods be applied to those areas which appear (by the scientist's intuition!) to be most profitably tackled. The inherent problems reflect the untold intricacy of the brain, the importance of ill-understood social factors, and the undoubted complexity of the nexus between them. But, eventually, critical scientific inquiries will lead to useful knowledge, a betterment of the human condition, and secondarily to a strengthening of psychiatry.

Psychiatry and Trust

There has been a decline in the influence and prestige of the medical profession as it has successfully prevented almost all the infective illnesses such as smallpox, tuberculosis and polio, but now finds itself of limited help before the Captains of Death in middle and old age – heart disease and cancer. Psychiatrists have none of the successes of general medicine to their credit, but some have put forward sweeping claims for their powers. These pretensions are being increasingly questioned both within and outside the profession. In particular, the public are less enamoured of their old image of psychoanalysts as 'magical helpers' who can interpret a glance, a gesture, a word, in terms of profound human psychology. No longer is the analyst credited with all the powers and charisma of a preternatural father.

And yet quiet progress has been made. Many types of therapy demonstrably alleviate patients' symptoms, so that the outlook for the more serious conditions is much less dispiriting than thirty years ago. The psychiatrist can often help his patients as much as, say, a general surgeon or a chest physician. In some ways the psychiatrist has more to offer. Coping primarily with patients with chronic illnesses with residual handicap, he has learnt to rehabilitate such human flotsam, finding them new jobs, new friends, new lodgings, and new hope.

Psychiatry is not a comfortable branch of medicine. Which other profession deals with illnesses swathed in such public ignorance, mistrust and horror? Which other profession lives with its patients in isolated, decrepit, understaffed lunatic asylums ('looney bins'), restoring their capacities only to return them to a hostile environment? Which other branch of medicine is provided with essential legal powers and is then scarified for using them? Yet patients are helped, real cures occur, people adjust in worthwhile and lasting ways. If society is dissatisfied with the care of mental patients, it could try financing psychiatric facilities properly instead of lavishing funds on more glamorous specialties. Society must decide its priorities. It is futile to elaborate costly procedures for safe-guarding the *rights* of mental patients while doing nothing to improve their *care*.

The Soviet problem encompasses a number of specific issues – the problems of diagnosis, the concept of responsibility, the right to refuse treatment, and so on. But it also accents the fragility of the bonds between psychiatrists and society. In the West, psychiatrists are typically somewhat more liberal and permissive than society itself. In Soviet Russia most psychiatrists have to withstand pressures to avoid being agents of an illiberal society. Unhappily, others actively spearhead their authorities' onslaught on political and religious dissension.

That is not only their tragedy but ours. For in the end all reduces to a matter of trust: trust between individual and society, psychiatrist and society, patient and psychiatrist. In the Soviet Union, trust is not plentiful but the need for it is dimly appreciated. In the Medvedevs' book, Professor A. V. Snezhnevsky is reported to rue the damage which the allegations of abuse were doing to Soviet psychiatry: 'Thousands of people, suffering from mental disturbances, would be afraid to turn to psychiatrists, as a result of which their health would be gravely jeopardised.' Just so, Andrei Vladimirovich, just so!

References and Further Reading

Chapter 1

LEWIS, A. J. 'Between guesswork and certainty in psychiatry'. *Lancet*, Vol. 1, 1958, pp. 171–5 and 227–30.

Chapter 2

ROGOW, A. A. *The Psychiatrists*. Allen & Unwin, London, 1970.

Chapter 3

LADER, M., and MARKS, I. *Clinical Anxiety*. Heinemann, London, 1971.

BELLAK, L., and LOEB, L. (editors). *The Schizophrenic Syndrome*. Grune & Stratton, New York, 1969.

NATIONAL SCHIZOPHRENIA FELLOWSHIP. *Living with Schizophrenia – by the Relatives*. Surbiton, London, 1974.

LADER, M. H. (editor). *Studies of Schizophrenia*. Headley, Ashford, Kent, 1975.

Chapter 4

Report of the Committee on Mentally Abnormal Offenders. Her Majesty's Stationery Office, London, 1975.

COOPER, J. E., and others. *Psychiatric Diagnosis in New York and London*. Oxford University Press, London, 1972.

SHNEZNEVSKY, A. V., and VARTANIAN, M. 'The forms of schizophrenia and their biological correlates'. In Himwich, H. E. (editor), *Biochemistry, Schizophrenics and Affective Illnesses*, pp. 1–28. Williams & Wilkins, Baltimore, 1970.

Report of the International Pilot Study of Schizophrenia, Vol. 1. World Health Organization, Geneva, 1973.

KENDELL, R. E. *The Role of Diagnosis in Psychiatry*. Blackwell, Oxford, 1975.

Chapter 5

SHEPHERD, M., LADER, M., and RODNIGHT, R. *Clinical Psychopharmacology*. English Universities Press, London, 1968.

AYD, F. J., and BLACKWELL, B. *Discoveries in Biological Psychiatry*. Lippincott, Philadelphia, 1970.

SZASZ, T. S. *Law, Liberty and Psychiatry*. Macmillan, New York, 1963; Routledge & Kegan Paul, London, 1974.

GOSTIN, L. O. *A Human Condition*. MIND Special Report, 22 Harley Street, London, 1975.

Chapter 6

SPRENGER, J., and KRAMER, H. *Malleus Maleficarum*. 1486; Folio Society edition, London, 1968.

MACDONALD, J. M. *Psychiatry and the Criminal*. Thomas, Springfield, Illinois, 1969.

DONNELLY, J. 'Legal aspects of psychiatry in the United States'. In Sim, M. (editor), *Guide to Psychiatry* (3rd ed.), pp. 1053–97. Churchill Livingstone, Edinburgh, 1974.

BERMAN, H. J. *Justice in the USSR*. Harvard University Press, Cambridge, Mass., 1963.

MOROZOV, G. V., and KALASHNIK, I. M. (editors). *Forensic Psychiatry*. International Arts and Science Press, White Plains, New York, 1970.

Chapter 7

SCOTT, D. J. R. *Russian Political Institutions*. Allen & Unwin, London, 1969.

SCHAPIRO, L. *The Government and Politics of the Soviet Union*. Hutchinson, London, 1973.

SAUNDERS, G. (editor). *Samizdat, Voices of the Soviet Opposition*. Monad Press, New York, 1974.

BUKOVSKY, V., and GLUZMAN, S. *A Manual on Psychiatry for Dissidents. Survey*, Vol. 21, 1975, pp. 180–99.

TOKES, L. *Dissent in the USSR. Politics, Ideology and People.* Johns Hopkins University Press, Baltimore, 1975.

Chapter 8

UNITED STATES SENATE COMMITTEE ON THE JUDICIARY. *Abuse of Psychiatry for Political Repression in the Soviet Union.* U.S. Government Printing Office, Washington, 1972.

Amnesty International Report. Prisoners of Conscience in the USSR: their Treatment and Conditions. Amnesty International Publications, 53 Theobald's Road, London WC1X 8SP, 1975.

Chapter 11

FAINBERG, V. 'My five years in mental hospitals'. *Index on Censorship*, Vol. 4, 1975, pp. 67–71.

Chapter 12

COOPER, D. *Psychiatry and Anti-Psychiatry.* Paladin, St Albans, Herts, 1970.

MEDVEDEV, Z., and MEDVEDEV, R. *A Question of Madness.* Macmillan, London, 1971.

More About Penguins
and Pelicans

Penguinews, which appears every month, contains details of all the new books issued by Penguins as they are published. From time to time it is supplemented by *Penguins in Print*, which is our complete list of almost 5,000 titles.

A specimen copy of *Penguinews* will be sent to you free on request. Please write to Dept EP, Penguin Books Ltd, Harmondsworth, Middlesex, for your copy.

In the U.S.A.: For a complete list of books available from Penguins in the United States write to Dept CS, Penguin Books, 625 Madison Avenue, New York, New York 10022.

In Canada: For a complete list of books available from Penguins in Canada write to Penguin Books Canada Ltd, 2801 John Street, Markham, Ontario, L3R 1B4.

Energy and the Environment

The Environmental Revolution
Max Nicholson

'Mr Nicholson is an ecological expert, a practical administrator, a prophet, a man with a splendid sense of history, and, best of all perhaps, a flaming, pamphleteering propagandist' – Michael Foot in the *Evening Standard*

Man and Environment
Robert Arvill

This is a book about man – about the devastating impact of his numbers on the environment and the ways he can attack the problem.

The Energy Question
Gerald Foley

'A very solid guide to the availability and use of energy' – *The Times Educational Supplement*

Fuel's Paradise
Peter Chapman

'As an introduction to the large-scale energy possibilities for Britain, Peter Chapman's book would be hard to beat' – *Ecologist*

Nuclear Power
Walter C. Patterson

'This book provides an important synthesis of the technical and political issues. It is excellent value and deserves wide readership' – *New Scientist*

Oil and World Power
Background to the Oil Crisis
Peter R. Odell

A searching look at the effects of oil production and consumption on politics and societies across the world.

There's Gold in Them Thar Pills

Alan Klass

Recent confrontations with many governments, principally over the prices of widely prescribed drugs, have brought the international drug companies into the limelight of public concern. As the extent of their monopoly and their profits became clear, these were justified by the companies' claims for the size of their research programmes.

But in this book Dr Klass has looked rather deeper into this defence. Too much of this research, he says, is devoted to manipulating chemical formulae to produce the same drug under another patent brand-name; too little is devoted to the serious problems, whether multiple sclerosis or cancer. Worse, an enormous investment in advertising has led to surrender by a majority of the medical profession: they prescribe ever more to achieve ever less.

Who is to stem the tide of new drugs, free samples and glossy advertising? Dr Klass believes that only the doctors themselves, backed by informed and articulate patients, can free themselves from the tyranny of the drug companies. Only together can they insist that health, not profit, is the target.

Pelican Mind Specials

Mind Specials are a series of illustrated books which look at some of the most urgent questions in the field of mental health. They are aimed at students, practitioners, and non-specialists with a particular interest in each topic.

Depression

Ross Mitchell

Depression is one of the most common contemporary problems. But what exactly do we mean by the term? In this valuable book Ross Mitchell looks at depression as a mood, as an experience, as an attitude to life and as an illness. He examines the organic, psychological and social roots of depression, laying particular emphasis on the early relationship between mother and child. His argument is illustrated by a number of case histories, and an important concluding chapter focuses on the role of both volunteer and professional in caring for the depressed.

Also published

Parents and Mentally Handicapped Children
Charles Hannam

Adolescent Disturbance and Breakdown
Moses Laufer

The Divided Self

R. D. Laing

The Divided Self is a unique study of the human situation.

Dr Laing's first purpose is to make madness and the process of going mad comprehensible. In this, with case studies of schizophrenic patients, he succeeds brilliantly, but he does more; through a vision of sanity and madness as 'degrees of conjunction and disjunction between two persons where the one is sane by common consent' he offers a rich existential analysis of personal alienation.

Sanity, Madness and the Family

R. D. Laing and A. Esterson

A classic of psychiatry.

Drs Laing and Esterson conducted a series of interviews with eleven patients who had been authoritatively diagnosed as 'schizophrenic': parents and relatives of the patients, in all possible combinations, were drawn into these interviews. The authors dramatically exposed the cross currents of affection, hatred and indifference within the family, frequently displaying the ugly sight of children being brainwashed by parents.

Their study throws doubts on the traditional view of schizophrenia as an illness with specific symptoms and its own pathology: it suggests rather that some forms of madness may largely be a social creation and their symptoms no more than the tortured ruses of a person struggling to live in an unliveable situation.